GETTING INTO

Childcare

working with children in the early years

JOANNA GRIGG

TROTMAN

Getting into Childcare
This first edition published in 2001
by Trotman & Company Ltd
2 The Green, Richmond, Surrey TW9 1PL

© Trotman and Company Limited 2001

British Library Cataloguing in Publication Data
A catalogue record for this book is available from the
British Library.

ISBN 0 85660 696 0

Typeset by Mac Style, Scarborough, N. Yorkshire
Printed and bound in Great Britain
by Creative Print & Design (Wales) Ltd

CONTENTS

ABOUT THE AUTHOR

Joanna Grigg worked with children in the UK and then abroad in a variety of other roles before having her own little darlings. Since then, she has juggled family life with writing careers books, training people in making careers decisions and running a community play scheme.

ACKNOWLEDGEMENTS

I greatly enjoyed going into such a variety of workplaces and meeting the people featured in this book, as well as all their little helpers. Many thanks to everyone featured, and others who gave me leads and background information, for all your help.

Joanna Grigg

INTRODUCTION

We are entering a new 'childcare era' in this country: it's as though the government has realised that parents need childcare and that although the system already in place is good, it's not extensive enough. So there's a lot of change in childcare, with all the work possibilities that brings with it. First, though, what is 'childcare'? It can mean different things to different people:

- To the working parent, it can mean anything that provides a safe environment for their child while they are elsewhere. This could mean employing a nanny, using a playschool, school, sports club, or other alternatives. The care may be solely play, solely education, or a mix of play and education, or it can mean time in front of the TV after a busy time elsewhere.
- For the child, it may mean cosy days with a grandparent or exhilarating days at a playscheme.
- It can involve work within
  - schools
  - homes
  - playgroups and nurseries
  - hospitals
  - offices and other workplaces
  - even a crèche within a theatre, and many other places.
- It means care of children of any age, but clearly there is more work available with younger children because as children grow, they need less supervision. Staff to child ratios therefore change, and in later years of childhood, most young people spend time without any supervision at all.
- Some people think the word 'childcare' refers to the less-structured care of children, such as an after-school club where children can choose an activity, or babysitting, or a care role with small children. Others also place education under the term 'childcare', though strictly speaking, children within a school curriculum are in education rather than care.

1

- Teachers and others often use the term 'early years' to describe pre-school education and care and then the first year of school (the reception year).
- For the government, whose priority is to free up parents to go to work, the childcare buzzword is 'wraparound' care. This means childcare provision from 8am to 6pm each working day, allowing parents to go to work. There is a big government campaign at the moment to get people like you interested in working in any of the childcare areas that contribute to wraparound care.

For you, looking at working in childcare, it's worth exploring all these areas and seeing which ones fit your skills and interests best. This book covers working in childcare in its widest sense, then directs you on to other research. It covers careers that allow you to work in a home environment, such as:

- childminders
- nannies

as well as in more structured environments:

- nursery and playgroup staff
- play specialists in hospitals
- teachers in nursery schools
- playworkers – and so on.

It has work that is suitable for those with no qualifications or plenty of qualifications, and for those just starting work as well as those coming back into the workplace. It doesn't cover people who want to work as teachers to the over-6s – these careers are covered in the book *Getting into Teaching* (see Further Information, page 77, under 'Teacher,' for details).

Each broad area of childcare work has its own chapter: these are listed under 'Contents' on page iii.

PARDON?

If you don't understand any word or term used in this book, look in the glossary at the end – from page 68.

BACKGROUND TO THE CHILDCARE SECTOR

This is a time of change in:

- people's expectations of childcare and work
- the structure of the organisations involved
- government policy
- training
- qualifications.

Why so much change? Because:

- Society is changing, and fewer and fewer parents now stay at home full-time to look after their children. This has caused a much greater demand for childcare places.
- People are more aware of quality issues in childcare. When your child went to playgroup once or twice a week, you weren't so bothered about what they did there so long as they were safe and happy. Now that many children spend substantial parts of their early years away from the home (or in their home but away from their parents), parents – and others - are more concerned about what they are doing. Is it play? Is it education? What is the best mix and at what age? And so on.
- People are also more aware of safety issues, and demand greater degrees of regulation such as checks on the people who are looking after the children, on the properties involved, on the safety of the activities and outings, etc.
- Research shows that a good start in life sets us up much better than a poor one. This is not exactly surprising . . . but many people feel that because parents often can't provide that 'good start' full-time at home with their children, then the care provided must improve and become more 'educational.' This will, they hope, produce adults who are skilled enough to keep the country competitive in Europe and the world.
- Government policy is taking these changes into account and bringing the age of entry into full-time school forward, as well as providing more state nursery places at earlier ages. It is also funding and encouraging after-school clubs and holiday playschemes to form wraparound care. At the time of writing, there is a big push to get

people interested in working in the childcare and education sector. Some people feel that some of the government advertisements are not representing the work properly, but are portraying childcare as child entertainment. 'It gives the impression that children are passive receivers,' says one childcare expert, 'which is not what working with children is all about. The slogan *Be someone to look up to* is nearer the truth. Children can almost fall in love with carers and put them on a pedestal. This has its drawbacks, but for children who don't have a lot in their lives, to have a friendly adult who doesn't tell them what to do (as their parents might or their teachers do) is a new experience – it opens up a whole new world for children.'

QUALITIES AND SKILLS YOU'LL NEED

It may sounds obvious, but you've got to like children. Some people think they'd like to work with children without actually having spent much time with them. You might work as a babysitter, for instance, and spend a little time in a one-to-one situation for a few hours, but the reality of working full-time with children is different. You won't know how different until you've tried it, so the message is: get out there and do some work experience to see if you like being with children enough to want to work with them.

Each chapter in this book lists specific qualities, skills and education that you would need to work in that particular area. To work with children at all you need to:

■ like children – see above;
■ like a challenge, be positive, reliable and adaptable;
■ be creative – both in activities, and in progressing your organisation and the children in it;
■ have a sense of humour;
■ get on well with adults as well as children. This might mean parents, other carers, professionals and volunteers;
■ have good organisational skills;
■ be flexible and able to change your direction within an activity, or in your career according to needs and external ideas;
■ have a huge amount of patience;
■ be a very calm person and at the same time be enthusiastic and bubbly.

PAY AND PROSPECTS

You are unlikely to get rich working in childcare. Most people do it because they love the work, but the reality is that the pay can be terrible, and is often insufficient. And it's not one of those careers where your earnings increase hugely when you qualify or gain experience, though they will rise.

The National Minimum Wage is helping childcare salaries, but there are still plenty of young people working in childcare who have to live with their parents as they couldn't live independently on the pay. Other people use their childcare income as a 'second salary' to help while raising their own families.

Many professionals in childcare and government are campaigning for better pay for childcare work. But it's usually parents who pay for childcare and it's already an enormous cost for most of them, so raising salaries is a difficult issue.

Because of this, you'll find it relatively easy to get onto a childcare course and into work, assuming you satisfy the minimum criteria. But as a nursery school owner says: 'People aren't going into nursery nursing because although it's perceived to be an easy option for girls, they find there's a lot more to it than they thought. With record keeping and assessments it's actually asking them to teach. If they've gone into it because they're not that academic themselves, that's putting them off, along with the pay. They don't get paid terribly well.'

If you need a better salary, become a teacher of early years children rather than a nursery nurse. You may be able to do this by starting off with nursery nurse training and using this qualification and experience to get onto a teaching course. You might be able to do this even if you didn't get very good qualifications at school. The right nursery nursing qualification can also be a way into other careers such as nursing. Childminding can pay well if you live in the right area and have a suitable home. If you are an entrepreneur, you may want to set up your own childcare business, a day nursery perhaps. But you will have to have experience and some money behind you first.

Pay is discussed in the relevant chapters. Whatever you choose to do, it's clear that experienced child carers are going to be in demand and that, if you're good, you will always be in work. So when you're researching your career and talking to people in the business, bear these things in mind and build a solid picture of what's out there, where you fit in and how you could progress.

MALES WORKING WITH CHILDREN

Everyone who contributed to this book wanted to see more males in these areas of work. One nursery teacher said: 'We'd love to have them. We just don't get males applying.' A day nursery manager said: 'It's impossible to get men. And I've heard some nursery managers say they would like to hire them, but daren't. This is because of the allegations that go around. A lot of people will look at men funnily when they pick children up from school, whereas they would never consider looking at a woman funnily, but the dangers are just the same.'

Anyone who works (or volunteers) with children is checked for previous convictions, but our prejudices run deep. The benefits for the children of having men care for them can be great: 'There are so many single parents around,' says one nursery nurse, 'that many of our kids have no contact with men at all. We do trial sessions for new children coming to the nursery and we don't allocate a key member of staff, we let the kid pick who they happen to like. Some of them don't like me because I have glasses, some of them don't like Adam because he's a bloke. They pick up on the silliest little things, so we just let them have a free rein for the first few months but you do notice that if they don't have men in their lives, they're quite wary to start with.' She goes on to say: 'Even though you're trying so hard not to stereotype any of them, the men do give a different type of play.'

Eddie works in a day nursery. He comments: 'I don't think there are men in childcare because of stereotyping – when people see men they think – oh yeah – men abuse children. When I've said I look after children I've had a few comments made that it's not quite PC. But 90 per cent of people do like it. I bring in male bonding; there are a lot of single parents who come in and see a male member of staff and think – excellent. I can provide that part that they haven't got with a partner. I'd definitely encourage other men to come into childcare.'

As the age range rises, so there are more men working with children. Youth work, for instance, has far more men within it than early years work. A local authority childcare worker says: 'There are more men involved in playwork and more still in youth work: it's cooler. It's often not seen as cool for men to work with young children, but youth work has street cred.'

LATE STARTERS

Many young people go into childcare work through one of the government training schemes. These are described in the next chapter (see page 10). If you're too old for these, you'll still be welcomed into any of the work areas described in this book: mature entrants are particularly sought after because of your experience of life and working with children.

SPECIAL NEEDS

Some children have learning difficulties and need additional help. The term for this is Special Educational Needs (SENs) and covers a huge range of difficulties from dyslexia through emotional problems, physical constraints, and beyond. About one fifth of children will have some SENs at some point in their early years and education. Only 2 per cent of children, though, have special needs requiring special schooling or additional resources outside those normally catered for in the mainstream school system. The government's policy of 'inclusion' is to integrate as many children as possible who have special needs into mainstream care and education, rather than run special schools and units where they are segregated. The degree to which this is achieved depends on resources, goodwill and the needs of the children involved, but can include financial help for carers to work alongside children full-time and one-to-one, or specially trained teachers being available for individual or group additional learning. It means that schools need to provide adequate additional learning materials and suitable access to buildings. It can include grants to playschemes to allow additional staffing, relief help for carers, and all sorts of other things. There are still special units devoted to the care and education of children whose needs prevent them attending mainstream care and education.

All child carers and educators will work with children with special needs in the mainstream system. Additionally, there are many career opportunities working specifically with children with special needs. If you're interested in this type of work, you need to make contact with organisations that can give you more information and some work experience. Look in the Further Reading section (page 70) for contacts.

SPECIAL CARERS

Working with children is physically demanding. In some people's eyes that means that having a physical disability precludes you from working in childcare areas, but this is not so. There are prejudices, but you won't find those among younger children, who are very accepting of people 'as they are.' One insider describes an incident: 'The children [in the day nursery] watched and listened to Chris and were interested. Then one of them asked him why he "spoke funny". He explained that he was hard of hearing, the child said: "Oh," and, satisfied, went off to play. That was the end of it.'

That said, you must be able to work safely and effectively with the children in your care. With young children, this probably means being able-bodied to the extent that you can catch a runaway before he or she reaches the gate, or kneel to clear sick from the carpet. This is less so with older children, and even with the younger age ranges the system can adapt if the will is there to do so. More workplaces and employers are recognising the importance and value in having a range of children and adults of all sizes, ages, sexes, colours and physical ability in together. As the scarcity of people working in childcare continues, even the less broadminded employers will need to consider employing those with disabilities. This may not be the ideal motivation, but if you can use it to your advantage and get the experience you need, then one of the major obstacles, finding initial experience and training, will be overcome.

Speak to your local careers service, who have an adviser who specialises in working with career searchers with disabilities, and will be able to help you get a placement in a good workplace. Also contact the relevant disability groups and seek their advice.

FURTHER INFORMATION

The chapter beginning on page 70 has listings of useful organisations, helplines, websites and publications, both general and specific to particular chapters, so once you've read a certain chapter look for relevant addresses in that Further Information section.

Chapter 1
TRAINING AND QUALIFICATIONS IN CHILDCARE AND EARLY YEARS

You can work in childcare without any qualifications as long as you satisfy the requirements of that workplace and employer (nursery, or family, or school, or wherever you want to work). You also need to pass a police check, to ensure you have no previous convictions that might present a danger to children, and a medical check to ensure that you don't suffer from a condition that could endanger children, such as certain forms of epilepsy. But if you want to get the better jobs, and progress as you gain experience, you'll need to think about getting some qualifications.

You can gain qualifications within education – at school or further education college or university, for instance – and also training qualifications while you are at work.

EDUCATION

Some courses and qualifications are geared towards a particular type of work, such as GNVQs (GSVQs in Scotland), which are General (or Scottish) National Vocational Qualifications. These are at two different levels, roughly equivalent to GCSE standard of study. There are also vocational A-levels (Advanced Certificate of Vocational Education, AVCE), which you take with or alongside A-levels (vocational A-levels are taking over from advanced level GNVQ). You can also take vocationally-slanted degrees and other higher education (university level) qualifications.

Once you know what you want to do, you can apply for a full- or part-time course that gives you the qualifications you need. These are described in the appropriate chapters (for instance, studying to be a social worker will be found in the chapter on social work). You'll have the chance to speak to teachers and tutors about your choices. Colleges have open evenings and some run events such as taster days, or buddy days where you shadow a current student. Colleges are also keen to attract mature students, and many will be developing more part-time courses to allow mature people to study more easily. It's a good idea to get hold of the prospectuses of all local colleges that run courses in childcare – if you do this right from the start, you can see what options are most practical. These will probably be sixth form, tertiary or technical colleges, or possibly private colleges. Look in the Yellow Pages or call your local Early Years Development and Childcare Partnership, EYDCP – see Further Information (page 70) for details.

TRAINING

Other qualifications are gained after leaving school or college and while you are working: these are training qualifications. Training means that you are already doing the job, and learning to do it, or some aspects of it, at the same time. This can be while you are actually doing the work (informal 'on-the-job training') or as formal training sessions run by your employer in the workplace, or in college on days off or in the evenings ('off-the-job training'). Almost all qualifications in childcare are now assigned an S/NVQ level (see below), to make the different qualifications more easily understandable and comparable to each other.

NVQs and SVQs

National Vocational Qualifications (NVQs) or, in Scotland, Scottish Vocational Qualifications (SVQs) are the standard way of describing what you have learnt in your work. They are not the same as GNVQs (GSVQs), which are taken in education - see above. They are vocational qualifications for people within childcare (and other industries and areas of work) or for those wishing to enter childcare.

S/NVQs are based on activities that you need to do at work, and they show that you can do your job well. You need some knowledge and background understanding of why various things happen, but S/NVQs mainly involve showing that you are competent in practical, work-based activities. Your abilities in your work are measured against a national standard starting at S/NVQ level 2 and up to level 4 (there is a fifth level but there aren't any childcare S/NVQs at level 5 at present). You can start at any level (depending on the level of responsibility in your job) and work your way up through the levels. The S/NVQ levels used within childcare are:

Level 2 – S/NVQs for people working as assistants or voluntary workers, working under supervision and with a limited range of responsibility

Level 3 – S/NVQs for those people who work under their own initiative, planning and organising their own work and supervising others

Level 4 – S/NVQs for those people in a managerial role in large or multiple settings, who carry out complex or non-routine tasks, or for managers with responsibility for quality control in a number of settings.

So you can see that S/NVQs apply to you when you are starting out, and that training and gaining these qualifications can take you into managerial work later in your career.

The organisations that arrange and administer the S/NVQs for childcare are listed in the Further Information section at the end of this book (see pages 72–73).

Accreditation of prior learning (APEL)

If you have been working in childcare and related fields but never used that experience to gain a qualification, you may be able to do this through APEL. This involves putting together a portfolio of evidence that may include training, qualifications and experience. You'll get support with this through your employer or through a training organisation, and an assessor will decide what previous evidence can be counted towards your S/NVQ. You can then build on what you have already achieved to complete the S/NVQ.

Training routes

There are government training schemes to help people train and work towards qualifications in childcare. For young people, these are:

- Youth Training (YT)
- Foundation Modern Apprenticeships (FMA – formerly National Traineeships)
- Advanced Modern Apprenticeships (AMA – formerly Modern Apprenticeships).

They are set up by employers in collaboration with training providers and organisers in your area, and they are in line with national training standards. Although you may be entitled to join one of these schemes, the popular schemes are harder to get onto, so to make sure you get the training you want, apply early. They are open to people aged 16 to 25; priority is given to those aged 16, 17 and 18. You are guaranteed a place on one of them if you are 16 or 17 and not in full-time education or work. In Scotland these schemes are called 'Skillseekers.' See Further Information (page 70) for people and places to ask about these schemes.

New Deal

This is a government scheme run through the Employment Service (via your JobCentre) for encouraging unemployed people back into work. There are different parts aimed at different groups of people (such as the long-term unemployed, or lone parents). Employers receive a weekly subsidy to help employ you, plus sometimes additional cash to help train you. You'll need to research current schemes by calling at your JobCentre or the information line/website – see the Further Information section, page 70.

Other training routes

There are other training routes (for instance, an employer may want to train you but not in the same way as these schemes suggest). There is a checklist used by the childcare organisations, so that they can see where any training fits against 'National Occupation Standards,' which are the training standards that have recently been set up within all these changes.

CHILDCARE WORK WITHOUT TRAINING AND QUALIFICATIONS

There will always be work looking after children, and there will always be employers willing to take you on without training you. This is OK if you are helping out during work experience, or doing some babysitting or something similar in the short term. (You should always ensure, though, that you are not left in sole charge of children in a workplace setting, such as a nursery or playgroup, and that if you are a young person babysitting, you follow guidelines and the wishes of both sets of parents – yours, and the child's).

However, good employers want:

- workers who care well for the children, and
- training schemes to produce good workers.

Hopefully all employers are now up-to-date with developments in training, but if you are offered work without a training scheme, or without a scheme that you can see fits into the framework, then think twice: it won't do you much good in the long term. Experience is crucial, yes, but you will increasingly need more training and qualifications if you are to progress, to enjoy the work and to earn more.

Some people don't ever want to, or aren't able to, gain any of the qualifications discussed above. Good employers will still value your work and will still encourage you to progress as you can and want to. Talk to your careers adviser about this.

Chapter 2
CHILDMINDER

A childminder looks after other people's children in the childminder's home. It's the most widely use form of daycare in this country and is a job for someone experienced in working with children, who enjoys being with them and who has a safe and comfortable environment for children to come to, usually when the parents are at work. Often childminders take some or all of the children they care for to school or nursery, then collect and care for them after the school day.

THE WORK

A good childminder does more than keep children safe. As in all childcare roles, you are in some ways a temporary 'parent-substitute' and need to be completely reliable, and to work with the parents, sharing information and strategies about the child to give a high-quality service. It doesn't mean placing the child in front of the TV all day: it means providing opportunities for the child to learn. Learning could be through ordinary domestic activities such as tidying up, through outings to the shops or to visit other people or groups, or through a structured game or other activity at home.

You'll also need to be registered with the social services department of your local authority so that parents can be sure that safety considerations and quality of care issues have been addressed. These include home safety, health and police checks. There is also an annual inspection. Recently, inspections have been taken over by OFSTED, the same organisation that inspects schools.

You might also be asked by the local authority to take a child for respite care because the parents cannot cope. In this case, the local authority would pay you.

CASE STUDY

Nicky has two small children and works full-time as a childminder to two other children. 'I have a 2- and a 4-year old of my own, and also care for a 3-year old and a 4-year old, though this lad is going to school full time soon and I'm not sure if I'll keep having him. If not I might take a baby; if I do keep the lad I'll probably also take another younger child, and build the numbers up that way as my own get older.'

She enjoys her work, though it is very demanding: 'There are days when I don't sit down at all, and days when the children aren't well enough to go to nursery but well enough to come here, and I can be chasing my tail all day. But when we're all healthy and happy it works very well. The children usually play happily together. You do have to be a step ahead all the time. If you have four small children all deciding they're bored at the same time, it's hell!'

She has the children from 7.30am until about 5.30pm. 'My husband is here for the first hour and our own children spend that time with him while I look after the others. When he goes to work, I get out an activity, perhaps a different toy or some art work. After a while we usually go out, either to the shops or to something like the church toddler group. If it's a playgroup or nursery day I drop whichever child off there and collect them later.

'I also prepare snacks and meals, and have to think ahead about food: I can't really go to the supermarket with them all so we have to do that at weekends. We do get odds and ends at the local shops all together though – they always like going shopping.'

Nicky thinks she'll continue childminding until her own children are at secondary school. 'Once they're more independent,' she says, 'I'll probably go and get a job, but at this stage, I love being at home with them all. It's interesting seeing how they all develop differently, and I'm really fond of my two "extras".'

QUALITIES AND SKILLS YOU'LL NEED

As well as enjoying their company and the activities children enjoy, you'll be patient, positive, encouraging and you'll create a happy and stimulating home environment where the children like to come. You'll form structured sessions where the children fit into a known routine, so you need to be an experienced and organised child carer. See the chapters on nursery nurse and teacher for an overview of the qualities you'll need.

You are a self-employed daycare worker, running your own small business, so you'll need to find your clients. (Although they will come to you from lists held by local organisations, you need to present yourself and your home environment attractively and demonstrate that the child would thrive there.) You also need to agree details with parents, making sure that everyone understands the arrangements, and fill in and sign a written contract. Other elements of the 'business' side of the work include keeping records for attendance, for first aid incidents, and for the financial side of things. You also have to sort out your own tax and national insurance, and arrange personal liability insurance.

TRAINING

Although you don't need to train or qualify, there is increasing emphasis on this and more support to help you train. And it's true that if you're qualified, parents and other professionals will see you as more committed and able. An NVQ has been developed at level 3 especially for childminders. This is the CACHE (Council for Awards in Children's Care and Education) Certificate in Childminding Practice (CCP). There are three units making up the certificate, so you can study at your own pace. You'll get a unit certificate for each part you complete but you need all three of these to gain the CCP qualification. You will be able to find details of local courses through the National Childminding Association (NCMA), or your local EYDCP. Any registered childminder can do this course without having any other qualifications.

HOW TO BECOME A CHILDMINDER

You won't be able to become a childminder until you've had plenty of experience working with children of the ages you plan to care for. This could be through nurseries, schools, playgroups or other organisations, or, commonly, after or while caring for your own children. If you care for a child aged under 8 other than your own in your own home you need to be registered, as mentioned above. Call your local social services department or your local authority office (such as your local EYDCP) for advice about childcare work. They will give you information about the registration process.

Initially, you need to pay a fee for registration and then fees for the annual inspection. You also need to pay for personal liability insurance, to cover you in case there is an accident involving a child in your care. There is currently a scheme providing start-up grants for newly-registered childminders in England. This is to help with the initial costs of preparing your home and becoming registered.

The same agencies will also tell you about training opportunities because, although you don't yet need to be trained or qualified, recent changes to encourage the growth of more, and better, childcare, include an increase in the number of training courses available. They will also give support services, such as referring you to a local childminders group and the NCMA – see the Further Information section, page 73.

HOW MANY CHILDREN CAN YOU CARE FOR?

When you start childminding you might be registered for only one child, and the age of that child might be limited. As you gain experience, you'll be registered for up to a maximum of three children under 5 years and a further three under 8 years. These figures include your own children.

HOURS

You can fit the work around your other commitments but many parents want wraparound care, and you could find yourself working long days to fit in with your clients. It's not a job you can necessarily just leave at the end of the day, either: if a parent is delayed, you will still need to look after the child. You'll also have to schedule holidays to fit in with parents' needs.

PAY

You'll be paid by each parent at a standard rate per hour that you set. This rate varies around the country, and even within areas it can vary a fair bit. In London, for instance, you might be paid up to £4 per hour per child, or possibly more; in other areas it could be as little as £1 per hour per child. Remember that you may have a number of children in your care at any one time. One recent childcare survey* puts average childminding earnings in London at £110 per child per week and in the North East at £75, with a national average of £89. You need to speak to other childminders locally to get an idea of what you might earn. Experienced childminders who build a good reputation are able to charge more.

CAREER OPPORTUNITIES

Many childminders love being at home with children and wouldn't want to do anything else. Others look after children alongside their own until their children go to school, perhaps, and then look for another type of work. Childcare recruiters are always keen to find responsible, experienced child carers to train into roles to suit their needs, and working as a childminder certainly gives you experience. Look through the other roles described in this book to see where this experience might lead you.

*Survey by the Daycare Trust, 2001.

Chapter 3
HOSPITAL PLAY SPECIALIST

It's very stressful for children to go into hospital, and they need plenty of support. Hospital play specialists give this support by working within the wards and the play unit (if the hospital is large enough to have one), playing with children and helping them to come to terms with what's happening to them through play activities. Hospital play workers are usually experienced nursery nurses who have retrained in this role (though some come to it through work such as art therapy). Larger children's hospitals may have up to 40 play specialists, while general hospitals with children's wards may have only a few. It's an expanding field of work. Hospitals are now built with specialist play units and older hospitals are converting space to house these units, as the importance of play becomes further understood.

THE WORK

You'll work as part of a team of play specialists, organising play and art activities in the play unit or in the wards. This play is planned to entertain the children, but equally will be aimed at helping them overcome fears, understand procedures, cope with pain and any side-effects of medication, and help in their development. You'll also work with parents and other children of the family, perhaps encouraging them to play together, or helping new friendships develop with other children in the hospital.

Another aspect of the work is supporting the medical staff and other professionals by assessing children's development through your observations during play. And on top of all that, you're the one they like the best because you organise their birthday parties!

In some areas, if a child coming into hospital is very frightened, the hospital play specialists will do a home visit first to play out any fears. They might use hospital and doctor sets of Playmobil and other toys.

CASE STUDY

Joyce is an experienced play specialist who now works as a hospital play coordinator within a children's hospital. 'The main aim of the play unit,' she says, 'is to look after the all-round emotional needs of children in hospital. We help them, through play, to understand and come to terms with illness, procedures and so on. For instance, we distract them with dolls – we have dolls that children can take blood from or put medicine into. We use books, too, to help them come to terms with what is happening.' Joyce and her colleagues promote the importance of play rather than have the children sitting doing nothing. 'We devise play programmes for our long-term children,' she continues. 'There's usually an aim for the programme, for instance, to get over a child being upset taking medication. And if there are any signs of abuse we are usually the ones to pick it up first because of the way the child plays. We all do a child protection awareness course and students cover this on the diploma course.'

Joyce also looks after her own ward, the isolation unit and oncology, and looks after training and coordinates staff. Part of the training she manages is teaching nursery nurse students about play and child development. 'We're all trained nursery nurses,' she explains.

'We're occasionally asked to do child development assessments.' Other work with professional staff includes attending case conferences with parents and social services, or other sessions with nursing staff and doctors. 'We work very closely with nurses, social services, and occasionally with health visitors if it's a little baby. Also with consultants, physiotherapists and speech therapists.'

Because the play specialists work regular, five-day weeks, they are consistent faces for the children in a hospital setting where most staff work shifts. It can be bewildering for a child to have a succession of different faces attending to their needs.

'It's a rewarding job,' says Joyce, 'which is probably why there are very few staff vacancies. We see children when they come in very sick and see them get better. We have no part in the medical process so we are the ones who get the smiles. When you help a child go through a procedure and you get a smile or laughter from the child at the end, it's always worth it.

'Children always remember the play person first. But it has to be something that you want to do: we do work with terminally ill children and not everyone wants to do that. We're there pretty much up to the end and some people can't take that.

'It's hard work – some days are really gruelling – I found it hard last year because we lost quite a lot of the children on the ward. We also get a lot of special needs children and even if you don't feel like smiling and saying, "hi, I'm the play specialist," you have to do it. The children don't want to be with anyone who isn't cheerful.'

QUALITIES AND SKILLS YOU'LL NEED

You need all the qualities of a good nursery nurse. In addition, you mustn't be squeamish. You don't need medical knowledge, but you do need to understand enough to know what you're talking about if a child asks you. You need a sense of humour, and great tact. Drawing ability is an asset: often, children will ask you to draw the latest cartoon figures.

HOW TO GET IN

'When a child falls sick,' explains Joyce, 'sometimes they regress, so you have to know what a well child is before you can treat a sick child. You need experience. We wouldn't take nursery nurses straight from their course without experience.' Also, having your own children gives experience to help with the parents, but this is not essential.

Once you are experienced, you need either to find a job and arrange to qualify while working in your new role, or spend 200 hours in a hospital placement then find a job. You'll need to speak with personnel departments in your local hospitals to see how they like to recruit and train their staff.

TRAINING

You need to gain a Professional Development Certificate in hospital play. The course is a level 4 equivalent, one-year part-time course run at colleges across the country. The National Association of Hospital Play

Specialists lists these courses on its website – see Further Information on page 74 for details.

Once you've trained, there's a registration procedure very similar to nurse registration. Hospital play specialists are registered for five years, then reapply for registration. You need to show evidence of, for instance, attendance at study days, as continuing professional training.

PAY

There is no nationally agreed pay scale though most hospitals start new hospital play specialists on a minimum of around £12,000, rising in the larger teaching centres and with promotion to between £15,000 and £22,000 for senior play specialists and play coordinators.

Chapter 4
NANNY

Nannies work in family homes looking after the children of the family, and sometimes of another family too in a 'nanny-share'. They tend to look after younger families, as many children move on to another form of childcare as they grow. However, some families keep their nannies, and possibly the same nanny, from when their children are small until they are independent. Live-in nannies live with the family and receive food and their own bedroom as part of their salary. Daily nannies live elsewhere and come into the family home each working day.

ANOTHER PERSPECTIVE: WHY DO PARENTS CHOOSE TO HAVE A NANNY?

Look at nannying from a parent's point of view, as this could give an insight into why you might want to do the work, and what you'd get out of it. Nurseries are often unsuitable for young babies, and the immediate choice for new parents is usually a nanny or a childminder (though more nurseries do now take very young babies). Once the child is older some parents still feel it's better for their child to be in the family home, rather than spend the week elsewhere. A nanny also gives the parents flexibility, as they can ask the nanny to work extra hours, or look after the child while they go away on trips. It also gives the parents backup when the child is ill and can't go to nursery. Nannies can also provide a relatively cheap form of childcare once there is more than one child to care for. Some families live a long way from anywhere and need a live-in nanny simply to get the children around – in which case they would provide a car for the nanny's use.

AND WHY MIGHT PARENTS CHOOSE ALTERNATIVE CHILDCARE?

There are various reasons why parents might prefer other forms of childcare, especially once their children are older. Employing a good nanny is expensive in many family's terms (though wage levels may seem low to you, it can still be a substantial cost to them). They might not want their child to become too attached to another person. They might not want to have a nanny living in the home with them. A childminder is a good alternative for some families, giving personal and constant care in a home environment without the family having to share their home with another person.

They might not trust one person with sole care of the child and instead prefer a place where there are several staff on duty. They may feel the child would benefit from more socialising with other children. They may have had 'bad experiences' in the past with nannies – this can be a difficult issue. Some families are very laid back about having another person in their home, others wouldn't want the crockery put back in the cupboard in any way other than the way they do it. This can cause frictions if the personalities of the nanny and family conflict, however lovely you all are as people. And of course, there are 'bad' nannies, and a family who has employed the wrong person in the past might not want to go through the experience again.

THE WORK

A nanny's job is to provide childcare in the safety and emotional comfort of the child's home and locality. This doesn't mean watching TV all day, for you or the child. In fact, you will hardly have time to stop if you are the nanny of a busy family. It involves providing the best care and development opportunities for the children in your charge, as well as helping to run the family home while the parents are busy at work or otherwise away. Your domestic duties should only involve the children: you'll cook and wash but only the children's meals and clothes, and you'll probably do some light cleaning but only of the playroom, toys, and children's rooms, say. With young children, this housework is part of the normal domestic routine and the child will be involved in all these activities with you, and learn through them.

Other duties may include taking and collecting children to and from nursery, school and clubs, socialising with families and children of the same age, helping with homework and children's problems as they arise and, very importantly, communicating fully with the parents about events and progress.

The nature of the work is similar in some ways to the work of a nursery nurse, and many nannies have similar qualifications. Yet the two jobs are worlds apart: the nursery nurse in a day nursery has a structured environment, regulated hours and adult company, supervision and help. The nanny is more or less alone. It's a job for someone who is experienced with children, confident and trustworthy.

THE HOURS

You will either 'live in' – which means living as a part of the family and having your home there – or 'live out', and go in on a daily basis. If you live in, your employers should be fair about giving you evenings off, and some weekends too, though in some homes you might find that time boundaries are blurred to suit the parents. If you live out you'll find it easier to keep to the contracted hours – if you're not there, no one can ask you to do a little bit extra.

Whichever way it is organised, you'll probably start early in the morning, perhaps helping the parents get the children ready for their day but certainly taking over in time to allow the parents to go to work. This could mean being on duty from 7 in the morning, or it could be later (or possibly even earlier!). You'll then care for the children all day, perhaps with time off while they are at school, and cook their evening meal. Then when the parents return, you'll report on your day and hand back to the parents. If you live in you will almost certainly do some babysitting and weekend work, possibly a lot. It you live out, this additional work will be by arrangement and you should be paid extra for it. Nannying jobs do vary enormously. Some families will ask you to do more than this and others, less.

WHAT'S IT LIKE?

It can be extremely hard work or can be much lighter in terms of workload, depending on the duties you agree with the parents, and the number and ages of the children. Some parents want you to have plenty of time to devote to the child's care and development, while others perhaps cannot afford to pay you for a full week and might ask you to share with another family, and that could mean different homes on different days or weeks, and additional work.

Handling the 'politics' of a family can be difficult. In some ways, you are a family member but in other ways you are 'hired staff', and getting the balance between being friendly and yet not expecting your employers to be your best friends, can be hard (for them, as well as you). It can also be difficult when you become close to the children you look after, perhaps closer, in some ways, than the parents themselves. It can be hard for the children, the parents and you, when it is time to move on.

A manager of a day nursery (who loves her work and can't understand why anyone would want to be a nanny) says: 'A lot of people favour nannying over the nursery business, they think they've got a lot more freedom that working in a nursery but they do get very bored. And of course people are scared coming into it now because of all the scary stories you hear.'

She's right – it can be boring being at home with young children without adult company, and this is something to consider. It suits people who are self-starters and will get out and about, as well as those who enjoy the company of children alone. It suits people who want that close relationship with just one or a small number of children. There is also the growing concern of safety in the home, and of recent court cases which have caused some people to consider whether it's a good idea to work as a nanny when accusations can be freely made. You certainly need to think about this, and all nannies should have public liability insurance and consider other cover. The Professional Association of Nursery Nurses (PANN – see the Further Information section, page 74) can supply cover to qualified nannies and has useful information about the nannying role.

WORKING ABROAD

Some nannies aim towards getting a job abroad, and there are some fantastic places to visit and experiences to be had as a nanny with a foreign or travelling family. If you are qualified and experienced you will be highly sought-after. However, remember that you are vulnerable: always use an agency to find a job abroad, as the agency will have vetted the employer. Some agencies specialise in foreign placements. You may not be paid very much, as your lifestyle may be seen as adequate payment. Also it can be difficult to make contacts outside the family if you are abroad and you may become lonely – speak to the agency about these points.

Others with nursery qualifications spend time as children's representatives with holiday companies. Here, the job is similar to working in a playgroup or day nursery, though there may be times when it's quieter and more like nannying. Generally, you will be devising and running a range of different and, increasingly, educational activities for holidaying children. The sessions are often short, perhaps two or three hours twice a day, though you may also take the children on day trips. It used to be that holiday companies employed anyone who liked children, but their standards have risen and the recruitment procedure is rigorous. That said, they are always looking for qualified, experienced people and it can be a great way to spend a summer season in the sun – or a winter in a ski resort. There is similar work in the UK. Contact the holiday companies for more information – find their brochures in travel agencies or go onto the ABTA (Association of British Travel Agents) website, where there is a listing of all their tour operator members.

CASE STUDY

Jane always wanted to work with children and left school after GCSEs, going to college to study for the NNEB (now replaced by the CACHE diploma). 'I liked the course,' she says, 'but there was more theory than I expected, and it was harder in some ways than GCSE work – our tutors made us work very hard. I liked the placements more than the theory: I did five different placements, including two families, where I worked one day a week with mothers and their children. I loved that, more than the nursery school placement as it was always so noisy there, and the children were hyped up a lot of the time. So I decided I wanted to work as a nanny.' Some of Jane's friends did go into work in a day nursery and enjoy it.

Jane was advised to get some experience before applying for nannying work: 'I didn't think I was ready anyway. I got a job in the day nursery that I hadn't liked so much and I still didn't like it, but I learnt a lot. Then I moved and worked for a year as an assistant in a nursery class. I liked that more even though the children were older, but I missed the little ones.' Jane learnt how to plan, monitor and assess the children there: 'It was very useful, far more useful that I thought it would be. It made me think more about planning activities and watching the children to see how they responded, than getting on with "plan B". But I liked working with small groups better than with a whole class, and I didn't really like the routine of school.'

Jane then applied through a nanny agency and went for interviews with families: 'I really liked seeing different home environments and there were two I knew I would be happy in. I chose the one closest to home, with three small boys, and I go in every day, I have a lot of freedom and really enjoy my work but most of all, I love having close contact with my special children.'

CASE STUDY

Martine is an experienced and qualified nursery nurse, who has worked as an au pair in America, in various nurseries and nursery schools, and now works a 'share' looking after two young children, one from each family. 'I like to move around, and nannying work is perfect,' she says. 'I get bored in one place for too long, but I tell people when I apply that I only want to work for a year, maybe two, and some families don't want a long-term nanny anyway.'

Martine has always been able to find work easily: 'I trained at a private nanny college, and people like that qualification, though the training is much the same in all good colleges.' She is also bilingual, and usually works with families who want her to speak French to the children at home. 'Where I work at the moment, one mother is French and wanted a French-speaking nanny. The other family think it's fine to have French spoken to their child, so it works very well.'

Martine works in one home one week, and then the other the next week. 'It can get difficult if the families aren't organised,' she says. 'I live out, and rely on everything being in place on a Monday morning. It usually is, though it wasn't to start with.' But she likes the variety this gives her working week. 'In fact,' she says, 'it doesn't make much difference where we are based as we like to be out as much as possible.' Confidentiality is always important for nannies, who have access to families' secrets, and especially so with a nanny-share. 'We need a lot of trust and respect, but we have that. I won't work for families unless they know what they are talking about when I first meet them. These families were very up-front about what they wanted and expected, and still are, and I like that. I am very happy here, but I plan to work abroad next.'

QUALITIES AND SKILLS YOU'LL NEED

As well as loving working with children, you'll need to:

- be able to get up early and keep good time;
- be organised, including being able to handle the children's expenses;
- communicate with parents, including 'selling' yourself at interview;
- have a clear idea of what you are doing and why;
- preferably be qualified (see below) but not necessarily: there are no police checks or inspections or registration to be a nanny – so if you can show you have worked in a place where checks are made, this will reassure the parents. Parents should always follow up references;
- have lots of good experience with children of the appropriate ages;
- be able to plan activities;
- plan meals, cook for, and feed your charges.

You may also need to hold a driving licence and be a confident driver; hold a first aid qualification and maybe others such as lifesaving; be open to the wishes of the parents in cultural, religious or family matters; and, sometimes, subtly help the parents with their own childcare skills.

HOW TO GET IN

There are many specialist nanny placement agencies, which will welcome you and find families for you to visit. They will not charge you for their services – if they do, go elsewhere. You will get a good idea of local salaries from agencies. There are government plans to regulate these agencies more fully, to try to prevent unsuitable nannies being placed with families, though only 30 per cent of nannies do go through an agency. Agencies have procedures to check you are safe, qualified and suitable for the job: it makes sense to go with an agency that takes time over finding out about you and your skills and experience. Not only does it mean they are serious about matching you with the right family, but also you know that they will have vetted the family for you. When the new Code of Practice comes into force, all approved agencies will carry out checks such as police, qualification and reference checks.

The remaining 70 per cent of nannies find jobs through newspapers, magazines and word of mouth. It is much cheaper for a family to recruit in this way, as using an agency will cost them a substantial fee. However, no one has vetted the family for you and you are in danger of being exploited; who, for instance, will negotiate and write your contract? There is also the safety aspect: remember never to go and meet a family or individual without telling your family or close friend where you are going and how long you will be. If the interview is in a hotel, do not leave the public areas of the hotel: if you are asked to enter a hotel room or if anything else feels 'wrong' then leave immediately and report it to the police.

When you apply to an agency or family or go to meet them, remember that they will be looking for someone who:

- has the best possible qualifications and work record, backed up by good references;
- has the right attitude to suit working in this way and to fit in with the family;
- has the personality to enjoy and excel at the work;
- understands children and wants to work with them.

They will get the right vibes from you if you project yourself well and communicate with them at interview, which shows that you will be able to communicate effectively with the children and with the parents too.

There are plenty of pointers towards performing well at interview: look at the PANN guide, 'All you need to know about working as a nanny', available direct from PANN – see Further Information (page 74). Remember that as well as meeting the parents, you will want to meet the children who will be in your care. You might also ask to speak to the previous nanny, if there is one, to get a 'feel' for the job.

PAY

All workers over 17 are covered by the National Minimum Wage, which means you must be paid at least £3.20 per hour if you are aged 18 to 21, and £3.70 per hour if 22 and over (£4.10 from October 2001). This doesn't apply to people who live and work in a family home. Salaries vary considerably, depending on the area, whether you live in or out, the hours, the perks (such as personal use of a car), and so on. You need to ensure that your employer pays your tax and national insurance; check whether this will be deducted from the figure they are offering you, or whether the figure is net (after deductions).

Here are some examples of weekly net pay in 1999, taken from the Nursery World survey of average salaries, printed in full in the PANN nanny pack (see Further Information for details of this pack):

Live-in, central London: lowest £150, highest £280, average £199
Live-in, other towns   lowest £110, highest £210, average £146
Daily, central London   lowest £170, highest £310, average £257
Daily, other towns   lowest £130, highest £260, average £195

It is possible, though unusual, to earn substantially more than this.

YOUR CONTRACT

You must have written terms and conditions of the work you are expected to do, the pay you will receive and any other issues. The PANN pack has a sample contract. It can be hard sticking to your contracted hours, as some employers may gradually erode your spare time. If it's not written down, you have no bargaining power. This is especially important with a nanny-share – it is usually better for you if you are employed and paid by one family, and the second family then pays a proportion of your wages to the first family.

EDUCATION AND TRAINING

There are no legal requirements for a person applying for a job as a nanny to be qualified. If you want to join PANN, though, you need one of these qualifications: CACHE Diploma in Childcare and Education (DCE), or NNEB Diploma (NNEB no longer awarded); BTEC Diploma; National Association for Maternal and Child Welfare (NAMCW) Diploma; NVQ level 3 in Childcare and Education. These can be seen as the industry 'standard' qualifications and parents like to see one of them. For more details on these, see the chapter on nursery nursing. Make sure before you start a course that the qualification is going to be sufficient for the work you want to do.

There are also three private residential colleges for nannies; details are in Further Information (see pages 74–75).

When applying for work, see whether your new employer will give you time off to train further, for example to gain a first aid certificate or go to college for further childcare qualifications. See if your employer will pay some or all of the fees.

CAREER DEVELOPMENT

Many nannies use their job to travel and work within a succession of new families and cultures; some prefer to stay at home, and a career as a nanny can be satisfying in its own right. Others use nanny training and experience as a base for other careers. For instance, the CACHE diploma fulfils the entry requirements for training courses in teaching, nursing, midwifery and social work. Or you may wish to work your way up in the nursery world, becoming a supervisor then manager, inspector, or specialist in special needs education. You might set up your own nursery.

Chapter 5

NURSERY NURSE

Nursery nurses care for babies and young children, usually up to the age of 8 but sometimes older than this. It's a role that combines the physical care of the child with helping the child to develop through play and other activities.

The physical side can be very hard work: it can mean keeping one or more small children or babies clean, fed and happy, or chasing after absconding toddlers, or being on your feet all day in a nursery school. The educational side is demanding too, and very important: research has shown that the high proportion of learning that takes place in a child's first five years of life speeds up later educational and social development. The work involves overseeing the developmental needs of each child and ensuring that the child is safe, happy and adequately stimulated.

WHERE YOU WORK

You might work in any of a variety of places with quite different roles. In fact, the term 'nursery nurse' can mean the work you do, or the qualification you hold, or both. Some people who work with young children have nursery nursing qualifications but their job is not called 'nursery nurse' (see for example Nanny, page 24, and Hospital play specialist, page 20). People who have this same qualification and work in day nurseries (see below) are more likely to call themselves nursery nurses. Here, you might work in private or local authority day nurseries, in nursery schools and classes, sometimes in primary schools, in playgroups or residential homes. You might also be employed in a specialist centre for children with special needs such as physical or learning disabilities. Children with special needs are increasingly attending mainstream schools, often with the support of a nursery nurse.

Nursery nursing in day nurseries

A day nursery is a pre-school for children ranging from small babies up to age 5, operating through the year and open long enough hours for the parents to work full-time. Many of the children who attend a day nursery may be there from 8 in the morning until 6 at night, five days a week for up to five years. Others may attend part-time, or may not start in the nursery until they are toddlers or older.

Some day nurseries won't take babies, as this specialised form of childcare requires a greater ratio of experienced staff to children. Many young babies whose parents work are cared for instead by nannies or childminders, who may also be qualified nursery nurses.

Many day nurseries are run as private businesses. Local authority day nurseries are set up in much the same way as private ones, though they are usually run in local authority premises for parents who work for that local authority. The fees are often subsidised, and the pay is generally better for the staff. Other day nurseries may be run as community ventures, voluntary schemes, or other patterns.

Changes in the way we all work, with more women at work full-time, have taken place along with the introduction of government subsidies to parents using day nurseries and other structured forms of childcare (through the nursery vouchers scheme). So there is a huge demand from parents for nursery places and, consequently, a great demand for nursery nurses to work in day nurseries.

Nursery nursing in other environments

As well as day nurseries, hospitals and nannying, all mentioned above, nursery nurses work in any environment where young children need care. This might be as an assistant in a nursery school (see the chapter on teaching, page 54), in a crèche in an office block or on a cruise ship, as a children's representative for holidaymakers' children (see the chapter on nannying, page 24): in fact, almost anywhere. Once you are qualified and experienced you'll find great demand, at the moment, in this country and overseas.

THE WORK

'Be aware it's not just sitting watching telly with them all day. Be aware that you're going to be responsible for the development of another human being,' says Sally, an experienced nursery nurse who works at a day nursery. 'We learn everything by example. You're trying to instil into them the way you want them to grow up. It is a huge responsibility, but it is one of the most rewarding jobs I think you can have. A lot of young people come here and say: I've baby-sat one child when they're asleep. Then they come in here for three hours, and they've got 24 kids roaring at them. A lot of young people don't realise the extent of nursery work. All the noise, and you're on the go the whole time – I don't think we sit down at all the whole day. You have to be constantly aware of what's going on all around you, and showing by example, with fairness, and things like that.'

Anyone who's worked with young children will have some idea of the demands they make and the care you need to give them. In a structured day nursery environment this will include receiving new children into the nursery and making them feel at home. As Sally explains: 'We take a long time settling them in and it makes their time here much happier.' Once the children feel at home, they join in the daily activities. These can include art, games, stories, drama, dressing up, outdoor play and sport, clearing up, cooking, music, and any number of other formal activities. As well as planning, setting up and leading these, you need to be aware of all the children during the activity, what they are gaining from it, any problems, friendships that are developing or being strained. You need to act where necessary, and also be able to stand back and allow each child to learn through experience.

So although many people see nursery nursing as a fairly low-key role, it is in fact highly demanding physically, emotionally and intellectually. That doesn't mean you need lots of high-level academic qualifications to do it (see the section on training, below), but to do it well you need to have a good brain and the motivation to use it.

There are many other aspects to the work, including a growing amount of child assessment and paperwork for 3-year olds upwards. This book can only give you first ideas: you really need to go into a nursery or other childcare setting and spend some time seeing what goes on.

CASE STUDY

Jane qualified as a nursery and primary school teacher in Brazil then gained plenty of experience there. She came to the UK, travelled around then started working as a nursery nurse in a day nursery, where she's been for nearly a year. 'I really like it,' she says. 'All the time I'm thinking about what can I do tomorrow with the children, if they're going to like this or that, what shall I do, what shall I change. You always do different and new things because you're working with people, it's not like an office job working with a computer. Being with kids is really great: you learn a lot from them, it's an exchange of ideas.

'It's not difficult, but it is hard. You deal with kids with different backgrounds and have to give special patience to each child. Each child has special needs, and you have to be very careful. You can do something with a child and the next one might not like it so you have to be very aware of the things that you're doing with them.

'It's physically tiring. You never stop, you work all the time, then you have to be there all the time paying attention. Sometimes the child behaves differently and you have to figure out if there is a problem at home, or we're not giving them enough confidence, or things like that.

'It's like every job: if you like to deal with kids and work with kids then you will enjoy it but if not, find something else.'

CASE STUDY

Tyna is an experienced supervisor in a large, busy day nursery and after-school club. 'I came here part-time with no qualifications,' she says, 'then when I became full-time I did NVQ levels 2 and 3. I would do level 4 now but I'm too busy at the moment.

'It's a love business really,' she explains. 'I don't think there's ever been a day when I haven't wanted to come to work. That's why I stay – it's a job that I think you can be really happy in.

'We have 18 staff here. I go and collect part-time children from schools at lunchtime, then at 3 o'clock I have a crew that goes out and collects the older children from the schools. We also have a music teacher come in, and a French teacher. We can have 60:40 qualified to unqualified staff. I try to get as many trainees in as possible, because then you're training them up to how you want them to work. If somebody's been here and finishes their course I quite often hire them, and I try to keep them as long as I can. I lose them to maternity leave, or to teacher training college because a lot of them decide they want to work with older children after they've been here for a while. I like a good age mix – I've got two grannies here, and three blokes: one runs the after-school clubs. All groups have one bloke and at least two girls and a couple of trainees.

'The one thing I miss is that I don't get so much time with the children, with little ones especially. There's so much paperwork to do now. It's a lot more for my girls and for myself: assessments, writing reports, progress, then we do school reports when they go up to school. The teachers at schools tell me they're so much further on because they can do so much here.'

Tyna explains one of the worst parts of the job: 'Sometimes we are so upset about children leaving. Once they go I won't see them again, and we're sobbing because we've had them for five days a week, from 8 until 6, for three years, much more than some of the parents see some of them.

'But it's a brilliant job, to be able to see a little 18-month old who wasn't able to put bricks together, then after a little while watch him build something and do a puzzle, and his pleasure in getting it done. I don't think there's any other job that gives you that kind of reward.'

QUALITIES AND SKILLS YOU'LL NEED

As well as the overall desire to work with small children, you need to:

- have patience, stamina, good organising skills, empathy;
- be a calm person, as well as very enthusiastic and bubbly;
- be able to encourage the children to be excited about things they're learning for the first time;
- be a responsible person and want that responsibility.

TRAINING

DCE (and NNEB)

The CACHE Diploma in Childcare and Education (DCE) is a standard qualification for nursery nursing, used by people working in many childcare areas such as nannying, day nurseries and playgroups, assistants in nursery classes, play specialists in hospitals, and so on. It has replaced the NNEB Diploma in Nursery Nursing. This is no longer offered by colleges although it is still valid if you already hold it. CACHE is the new Council for Awards in Children's Care and Education, which has taken over from NNEB. The DCE qualification is at NVQ level 3. You take it full-time at college, and the course lasts two years. You need at least two GCSE passes at grades A–C, or equivalent, to do the course. Contact CACHE for a list of all colleges offering this. You can also study it part-time, and CACHE also offers other courses.

Another two-year course is the BTEC National Diploma in Early Years (previously known as the BTEC National Diploma in Childhood Studies). Again, this qualifies you to work as a nursery nurse; it is slightly more academic and requires four GCSE passes grades A–C, one of which should be English Language or Literature. It is also a level 3 qualification. Some students go from this into higher education to train as teachers, nurses or social workers. Note that BTEC is now called Edexcel, though the term 'BTEC' is still commonly used, as is 'NNEB' (see paragraph above).

Although the DCE and the BTEC diploma are the more usual qualifications, there are others, such as:

- privately run Montessori Centre courses, teaching a different approach to childcare;
- NVQ training qualifications, such as Tyna's (see the case study on page 37). An example might be the City & Guilds Early Years Care and Education at NVQ level 2;
- NAMCW (National Association for Maternal and Child Welfare) Certificate or Diploma.

There are more of these. If you start with a level 2 qualification you may then want to work towards a higher level qualification.

As there are currently many changes in childcare qualifications and the bodies awarding and administering them, it's best to do your own research. Talk to the staff at your local College of Further Education's open day, look at the prospectuses, send away for details from awarding bodies (addresses are in the Further Information section) and speak to people where you do your work experience.

Note that full-time college courses include placements in childcare centres: this might mean two days a week in various placements throughout your course.

In Scotland there is a two-year SCOTVEC National Certificate in Caring Services (Nursery Nurses). See Further Information for contact details.

PAY

Private day nursery pay starts at about £8000 per annum for a trained nursery nurse, rising to about £10,500. Councils, universities and hospitals pay about £9000 upwards. Nursery managers earn up to £14,000 or £15,000. Salaries are higher in London.

These pay levels mean it's not possible to live away from the family home in many parts of the country, so you may have to stay with your parents. This is one reason why people choose to become live-in nannies.

GETTING IN

'When you decide to do something, you don't need experience first otherwise you'll never get in there. You have to start, but when you start you have to make sure this is what you want to do and this is what you like to do.' This is Jane's view (see profile on page 37). It's certain that you need to get some unpaid experience in a nursery before you make a commitment to a course – if you start a two-year training course without any real exposure to the work, you could waste a lot of time. Once you have this, and have spoken to people within the nurseries, contact the colleges and go along for taster days or open evenings. Colleges try to get as many people into courses as possible and if you have the required qualifications and some experience you'll find it easy to get a place. Your work experience while studying will give you plenty of contacts: many people go on to work at the places where they trained.

Chapter 6
PLAYWORKER

What a wonderful job title. And it really exists! It involves working with children aged 5 to 15 outside the school environment in a project set up by one of many different types of organisation, from the local authority, through to charities, special needs and community groups. You may be one of a large team running a holiday playscheme, or the sole playworker in a community centre welcoming families, or in one of many other environments. What is sure is that as a playworker, you'll be giving children the opportunity to play in their own way, safely, fairly and in a caring environment.

THE WORK

We tend to think that play is just something that children are allowed to do once they have finished their homework. It's easy to forget that play is essential in children's development: it allows them to experiment and learn about themselves and other people, and allows them the choices that they rarely encounter in school or sometimes at home. A playwork environment can appear to be unstructured, as children are often able to choose which activities they do and when, and go from one to another, or even do nothing at all. In fact, a good playwork setting is planned and administered to allow this freedom of choice while also giving children the opportunities to play in ways they might not anywhere else, and will allow them to develop in their own way, at their own pace. This means involving the children and young people in planning and even running the play setting. Working together in this way encourages new relationships with carers and other children and sometimes with parents, and develops those relationship skills for the future.

Playworkers aim to help build children's self-confidence, the ability to choose, relationship building, fairness, care for others, and any number of other skills from physical and coordination skills to specific activity skills, through to greater awareness of themselves and others.

QUALITIES AND SKILLS YOU'LL NEED

You'll need to show an understanding of the role of play in development and that you have worked with children/young people in a play context. If you are applying for higher education courses then refer to the UCAS handbook (see page 78) and other guides for entry requirements.

Overall, you need to love working with children in what can be a demanding role without the structure of some other childcare environments. If you enjoy the challenge of the unexpected, of thinking on your feet, of being aware of children's needs, when to intervene and when to stand back, know how to chat and draw children into play where appropriate, and have a range of other skills using your natural and learned empathy and understanding of people of all ages (you will need to develop relationships with adults as well as the children and young people), then this could be for you. Playworkers find it exhausting but challenging and great fun.

Many people who have their own children find a second career in playwork; it is also a progression for people already working with children in areas such as nursery daycare, and welcomes young people and those new to play as a work area.

CASE STUDY

Jane is a Play Development Officer for a local authority. She came into this job after many years of experience with children in various areas, including playwork. 'It was difficult to get a full-time job in childcare,' she remembers, 'so I mixed and matched: I worked in schools, making festival dragons, for instance, then I finished there at 2pm, raced to another school and collected three to six children to look after. Then a couple of evenings a week I did youth work. This was until I was lucky enough to get a full-time job with the council as a playworker.'

The local authority play unit where Jane works operates most of its activities in the school holidays. 'Our focus is to provide child-centred activities for children aged 4–14, in a variety of ways', she explains. 'We use play development to achieve this. There's very much a child-centred approach to participation – they build their social, physical and development skills naturally through playing. It's about what a child wants to do as opposed to what an adult needs – it's about choice, and the child can choose.'

The play unit sets up and runs activities such as playschemes, children's fun days, children's activities in the park during the summer and activity days in places like museums. There are also sports, arts, drama projects, astronomy clubs, and IT clubs, with drop-in facilities for older children. The unit sometimes works with youth clubs, or might hire a community centre and set it up for a week. Then they move the activities around so that children in one locality can experience a variety of activities. 'Where we can, we work in areas of highest need as well as providing universal services,' explains Jane.

Most playworkers are temporary and work part-time. 'There aren't many avenues in terms of playwork,' says Jane. 'Playworkers can be a mix of students, older people, and those who want to make playwork or youth work their career.' She recruits people for the many activities run by the play unit. 'We look for previous experience with children, from pre-school to youth work. We also like specific skills in the arts, sports and drama, and someone with a good basic foundation in play: they've got to have some experience. A whole range of people make up the team. It's an opportunity to input their own ideas; in training we will take a group of workers and get them to think of scenarios, such as having a group of 20 children for three hours – what would you do? We look to see if the activities allow children to take things their own way, and aren't prescriptive, that they let the children see some things through and take risks without jumping in. It's not "I'll draw that for you" but "Here's a pen". It's about facilitation. Children who are good are encouraged but the children who are not so good are also encouraged.'

PAY AND CAREER DEVELOPMENT

Local authority playworkers are paid from around £6.00 an hour, and it's all temporary work. If you persevere you may find work running a centre, and so gain more experience that way, and your pay will reflect this. But, as Jane says: 'Playwork is undervalued and very poorly paid. People don't see it as a proper job.'

Opportunities for full-time employment are few, but you can fit part-time work in with your own personal development or other work.

TRAINING IN PLAYWORK

There are diplomas, degrees and postgraduate courses available in playwork, which you can research through your careers officer or the UCAS handbook and university guides. See the SPRITO and Playwork websites or call them for more information. Once you have a job, you will be trained as necessary to do that work.

GETTING IN

Contact your nearest National Centre for Playwork Education (see SPRITO website for details) for more information. Find out what training schemes operate locally by calling your TEC/LEC. Also try your local authority and ask to speak to someone in the Play Unit or EYDCP, who will direct you on. You can also speak to your careers teacher or adviser about this, and use the careers library to gather more information.

Chapter 7
PRE-SCHOOL VISITOR

Part of a child's development comes through play, where discoveries of the world, people, relationships, and all sorts of other things, are made. But some parents don't play with their children, for all sorts of reasons, so pre-school visitors offer to go into their homes and spend time with the parent and child or children, to help with activities that the child will later continue in playschool and beyond. The role involves working with a parent alongside a child, and visitors need to have experience, empathy and initiative. For instance, although not strictly what visitors are there to do, there may be times when the visitor has to think 'OK, the mother needs a break here' and play with the child while the mother gets a chance to just sit and observe the play and join in when she feels ready. Visitors also help with parenting skills. Pre-school visitors are employed by social service departments and work school hours, to fit in with families.

THE WORK

'We're not going into parents' homes and telling them what to do,' says Jan, an experienced early years playworker who now manages a home visiting scheme. 'The role of the visitor is not to be a teacher or adviser, it's more about modelling than teaching.'

Visitors work independently, though you probably won't go on a first visit on your own as you won't know what you're going into. 'We won't know anything about the family's background,' says Jan, 'so you need a very acute sense of personal safety. The training reflects that.'

You'll also be trained in 'boundaries': knowing what you can do in your visitor role and when you need to discuss things with your line manager. Sometimes a family can become very dependent on you, maybe ringing you at home or inviting you to family celebrations. But the role is professional befriending and there have to be boundaries. Again, the training covers situations like this and how you would cope. It also looks at child protection and how you might alert other agencies that there was a possibility of child abuse, though this can be a very fine judgement sometimes, especially when working with families from other cultures and differing lifestyles.

QUALITIES AND SKILLS YOU'LL NEED

You don't need qualifications, though most people who go into this work do in fact have one or other of the childcare qualifications. You do need to have cared for children 24 hours a day, as a parent or other carer such as an experienced live-in nanny, so that you understand what it's like to be a parent. If you have solely nursery nursing experience within a day nursery, for instance, you'll know what it's like to have children for eight hours a day and then go home, but not how it is to live with them.

You also need personal warmth, and to pass the 'doorstep test,' as Jan puts it. How you come across initially can make all the difference to whether a family accepts the visiting service or not. You need to be a warm, caring person with real empathy, qualities that are more important than technical skills such as knowledge of the Children Act, which can be learnt through training. You also need a sense of humour and of approachability, and to have a relaxed approach to families. You need to be non-judgemental, with a degree of assertiveness in situations where boundaries are important and where you may have to speak out to deal with something without alienating the family. You'll need self-confidence and an ability to think on your feet in sometimes very challenging situations.

PAY

There is a standard pay scale and visitors earn about £14,000 pro rata, upwards.

CASE STUDY

Christine has her own children, and works as a part-time pre-school visitor for children aged 18 months to $2\frac{1}{2}$ years. 'It's nice job,' she says. 'It was difficult at first, but once I'd done the first couple of visits it became easier. It's difficult if people's standards are different from your own, but once you've seen it all, you're more concerned with the child and the play.' She explains how research has shown that children who have been visited at home in this way are more confident and ask more questions when they start at playschool, because the activities are not all new to them. 'It's a nice job – and you can go on days out, in the summer for instance, on a coach or to the beach.'

Certain areas of Christine's home town are designated for pre-school visiting schemes because of the social needs of the areas, but any family living in the area can ask for a visitor for up to a year, regardless of income. Christine has other responsibilities too: 'I also run groups and introduce parents to other parents so that they're not so isolated. I help run a women's group for mothers with mental health problems. The child goes into the crèche and the women have two hours to talk together and with someone from MIND (the mental health charity). It's very interesting.'

GETTING IN

There is a national network of agencies called Sure Start, set up to help children under 4 and their families so that they are ready to flourish when they start school. It brings together health services, early learning and childcare, and support for parents. Jan and Christine, featured above, both work for Sure Start programmes. By 2004 there will be 500 local programmes in disadvantaged areas. Look at the Further Information section for more details of the work and how you can apply.

Chapter 8
SOCIAL WORKER

Some children have a difficult path through their early lives and need the additional support of people who work as social carers or social workers. These people work for agencies such as local government departments or charities or sometimes private companies. Social carers and social workers who work with children have a main priority, and that is to focus on the best interest of the child, listen to the child's wishes and feelings and, taking age and circumstances into account, act towards achieving the best solution for that child. This usually means trying to keep families together, as most children want this. Sometimes, it's impossible to leave the child with the family and, usually with the parents' consent but sometimes empowered with a court order, the child may be placed in local authority care, with continuing support to the child and the family from the social workers involved.

'Social work' means work done by professionally qualified people called social workers. This and many other roles are more loosely termed 'social care.' You'll start out as an unqualified carer. You may remain in one of these essential roles, or may move on to become a qualified professional social worker, but before you do that you'll need voluntary experience and that will be through social care work.

SOCIAL CARE WORKER

There is always a demand for people to work in jobs within social care. This might mean working in a children's home, for instance, or supporting a child with special needs within a school environment. While you won't need to be qualified for this type of role, you will need to show high levels of care, respect and dignity to your clients in all your work. There have been cases of abuse within children's homes recently brought to court, as well as other failures of the system that was put in place to protect children, and because of this many sectors involving children are being more tightly controlled. The Children Act of 1989 made many changes, and in some places the spirit of these changes wasn't evident. It's clear that if you enter these fields, you need to understand what is required of you, and that you will need good supervision and training, with an underlying core of support available to you at all times.

Some of these care roles move towards work in other sectors. For instance, playschemes may require social care support workers, perhaps specifically to work with one particular child, but playwork is another field of work in itself and is looked at in Chapter 6 (see page 41).

CASE STUDY

Pari works as an assistant in a local authority family resource centre. 'I've been working here for four years. Before that I trained as a community interpreter, but that was part-time. I liked having contact with families through interpreting so I applied to work here.' The Centre is run by a team of social workers, and supports families from many cultural backgrounds who need a place to be, who need resources such as furniture or equipment that has been donated, or want to talk to a social worker. 'My languages are very helpful,' says Pari. 'I speak three different languages and can be an interpreter if I am needed, but my main work is talking to families who come in, and seeing if I can help them. If they need help from social services, or another agency, sometimes I have to refer them to one of the social workers, but often I can help them myself.' Pari might see how they are getting on as a family by asking after the children, and how they are doing at school, and so on.

'Often, newcomers to this country have problems fitting into the new culture, and their children start behaving differently. Some parents find it hard to adjust, and to know how to deal with their children. I talk to the children too, and we share and laugh a lot – it's a place people come to relax as well as solve their problems.' There are increasing numbers of centres like this, many of which also provide training for adults. Pari would like to continue his career in this field: 'I hope to gain an NVQ,' he says. 'We are looking at setting up a training scheme for this.' In the meantime, he has ongoing training and assessment, and support from the staff at the centre.

QUALITIES AND SKILLS YOU'LL NEED IN ANY SOCIAL CARE ROLE

You must want to help people, and enjoy working with them. If you're not interested in people then it will be a gruelling and frustrating struggle. And 'people' means adults too, because social work with children involves working with families, carers, colleagues and other agencies, not simply with the children themselves. You'll also need to:

- be a good listener, without getting impatient or angry;
- undertake some training;
- be mature, and able to 'bounce back';
- have a good sense of humour;
- respect other people, empathise, and not blame them for their situation;
- be patient and committed;
- forget your clients' problems at the end of each day.

SOCIAL WORKER

Children's and families' social workers are professionally qualified, and help children and families with the same sort of needs as outlined above. You could say that they are a type of therapist – they listen, and try to offer solutions to people's problems. But they are also working within a social care system with rules, regulations and limited resources, and they act as providers of these services to the people who need them most. This can mean assessing clients (or 'service users') and finding the right help for them, or if this help is not available, explaining this and trying to support them in other ways.

As a social worker, once you've assessed the needs of your client you will then 'buy' the service that your client needs. That means arranging and costing the care package you feel is appropriate, and making sure it sits within your budget. Some social workers, more often those working for a charity, provide the service of care themselves, rather than arranging this with another agency.

CASE STUDY

Beth, a qualified social worker, is an educational welfare officer (EWO) in a large city. She works for the Local Education Authority and is part of the team that deals with the social problems children and families encounter within school education. 'My role is very much a support worker,' says Beth. 'I work closely with and support the schools in my patch, and have regular meetings with a representative from each. We review the caseload and keep each other informed of what's going on.' A problem might be a child suddenly underachieving, and the form teacher being unable, through talking to the child, to work out why, then referring the case to the school's welfare teacher. 'Quite often, social services already know about that child's problems,' explains Beth. 'For instance, the whole family may be having problems because the parents are substance abusers, or one of the parents has left the home. It can be very distressing to see how this is affecting individual pupils in the schools.'

Beth must work closely with the children, the schools and people in other departments: 'Sometimes there's an obvious answer, and we can procure the right services immediately, such as re-housing the family. Often, though, it's a long process of working and reviewing, and trying to relieve the stress on the child.' Beth might have to appear in court: 'We may need a court order, or I may have to give evidence if the police are involved, or explain what we are doing to help, which might allow the courts to decide the best course of action.' Beth also works closely with educational psychologists and other professionals.

QUALITIES AND SKILLS YOU'LL NEED TO BE A SOCIAL WORKER

As well as the qualities listed above, which are needed for any sort of social care work, you need to be numerate and able to work out the best 'deals' and care packages for the people in your care. You need strong administration and ICT (Information and Communications Technology) skills, and academic ability to get through the professional exams. You need to understand and fully know the legislation, always keep an open mind, be accountable for your decisions, be able to present your case clearly and convincingly and be calm in stressful situations. It is very challenging work: you need to be able to juggle demands from different people and agencies, and stick to your guns when it gets tough convincing people. You may feel overworked and under-appreciated, and you still have to keep going. You need special communication skills for working with children, in particular the ability to listen. You also need to be able to work well with other people in your department as well as those in other agencies.

GETTING IN AND MOVING UP

Before you can train as a social worker, you need experience. This might be through social care work, but most people start with voluntary work. This could be in any area. You might start working with a playscheme, see the specialist support assistants working with certain children, and want to move into working in that area. Or you might go into a children's residential home as an ancillary. You may have specific ideas about your future career but be unable to find exactly the right voluntary experience; however, this probably doesn't matter – employers understand that it's not always straightforward. They want to see a commitment to the work, hopefully in a variety of roles, and they want to hear what you thought of it, what you have learnt, and how you want to proceed with your career in the light of this experience.

Volunteers are essential in the social care sector, but that doesn't mean organisations will take just anyone prepared to try the work. The selection procedure can be rigorous – indeed, it *should* be rigorous – and if it isn't, perhaps you should be asking why. Also, as already mentioned, you should receive some training before you start.

Try contacting your local Citizens Advice Bureau or Volunteer Bureau for local volunteering ideas. There is also a national helpline for volunteers run by Community Service Volunteers – see Further Information, pages 76–77. You might also approach private day nurseries, playschemes or a children's hospice.

Your voluntary experience will give you a far clearer idea of where you want to work, and the contacts you make will help you decide on the education and training you need. It's a good idea to start voluntary work as soon as you are old enough: even if you can't find exactly what you want while you are younger, your CV will look better, and you will have built up a good idea of what you want to do and the experience of how to do some of it, before you need to make all your educational decisions.

TRAINING IN SOCIAL WORK AND SOCIAL CARE

Most social workers work for the social services departments (SSDs) of local authorities, and most people they take are qualified with the Diploma in Social Work (DipSW). This is a two-year course, entailing both academic study and work placements. You can specialise in work with adults, or with children and families, though once qualified you can move between these areas. You can do the diploma as a non-graduate, at university or as a postgraduate. There are courses around the country, and you can study full- or part-time. Another route to social work is via the Open University's (OU's) Foundation Module. The OU also offers a DipSW course. The number of ways in is complex and confusing, and is getting more so, as social work training and qualifications are being reviewed. You'll need to research this for the areas you're interested in.

Most jobs within SSDs are in the larger cities. As well as applying for work in SSDs, you can look out for jobs with national charities and voluntary organisations, and local organisations. You'll need to look at the weekly newspaper *Community Care*, other more specialist papers relevant to your area (such as the monthly *Young People Now*, and *Youthwork*), as well as advertisements in newspapers such as *The Guardian* on Wednesdays, *The Independent* on Thursdays, the local press, and so on. You'll find employers of social workers in the *Social Services Year Book* in your reference library.

After a couple of years' experience you might want to do more professional training and work towards a PQ (post-qualification) and advanced award. You may want to keep contact with clients as you progress, and so become a 'senior practitioner,' or may wish to move into management. There are good career structures available within professional social work. NVQs/SVQs are available to people already in social care or social work, up to level 4 – contact your local careers office or your local Training and Enterprise Council (England) or Council for Education and Training (Wales) or Local Enterprise Company (Scotland) or Training and Employment Agency (Northern Ireland) for details.

PAY

Qualified social workers earn between £16,000 and £25,000 a year. Unqualified social carers earn anything from the minimum wage upwards, though this may be augmented with allowances for unsociable hours.

Chapter 9
TEACHER OF EARLY YEARS CHILDREN

We'll always remember our teachers – they guide or drag us, happily, or kicking and screaming, through our school years. Some are wonderful, others perhaps less so, but they are fundamental to our education – they help give us that base we need to get on with the rest of our lives. Think how much more this applies to teachers at nursery level, where the children coming into nursery school are still relatively unformed. Some may barely be speaking, or may not have learnt to socialise; others may already be good readers. All these children mix together in the standard nursery class, and as a teacher you have the opportunity to help them develop, in every respect, into 'themselves.'

WHAT IS A NURSERY SCHOOL OR A NURSERY CLASS?

It is a place run by or staffed by nursery teachers, among others. Although some day nurseries call themselves nursery schools, they're not unless they have a teacher on their staff. Day nurseries can provide excellent early environments for the very young – it's not a case of 'only a day nursery.' But they are different.

State nursery schools, along with their equivalent – nursery classes attached to primary schools – form the first tier of our formal education system. There is a set curriculum, with aims and outcomes to be planned and recorded, reports to be written and progress to be monitored and discussed. 'But the main aim of the nursery school,' says Liz, head teacher of a nursery school, 'is to provide children with a happy educational experience as a separate phase of their development. I don't see it as just pre-school, as if it's just a big preparation for school – it's its own time. Children should be self-confident and able to make choices and able to socialise. I think they're ready for what comes next if they can do this.'

THE WORK

As a nursery or early years teacher you'll receive children aged 3 or 4 into the nursery school or class and settle them until they are used to being apart from their parent. (This may take a long while and involve gradual separation until the child is happy.) You'll assess each child's previous learning from watching, conversing and playing with the child, and record this. You'll monitor each child as you teach through each term, completing forms that ask standard questions about each child's progress. And you'll despatch the children into primary education once they are ready to take up their places. But, says Liz: 'The main thing is that they should have a sense of awe and wonder in everything they do.'

CASE STUDY

Helen is a qualified and experienced early years teacher. She trained in primary teaching and worked for several years teaching reception and year one children, before getting her current job in a nursery class. 'I just love small children,' she says. 'I enjoy being with all children, but when they first come into the class, they are so eager to learn and ready to absorb new experiences.'

It's not always this straightforward. 'We get children from many different backgrounds, and that can be challenging,' Helen adds. She explains how it can be at the beginning of a school term: 'Some of the new children are worried being here. They might not have been in a group environment without a parent or carer before, or might have been in a playgroup that didn't have much structure to it and they feel overwhelmed by larger groups. Others will be very confident and ready to socialise. We have identical aims for all the children in the targets the government sets, but individual aims for each child based on how they are when they arrive. For one child, getting through the session without hitting another child can be an achievement. For another, it might be holding a pencil for the first time. We plan and structure our activities very carefully, and maintain a controlled, peaceful and creative environment, while at the same time being aware of each child's needs and supporting them through each session. It is non-stop energy, but non-stop interest too – I never, ever, get bored, though I do collapse exhausted after a particularly demanding day.'

WHAT IS THE DIFFERENCE BETWEEN A TEACHER AND A NURSERY NURSE OR ASSISTANT?

There may be marked differences in the work of qualified teachers and other staff in a nursery school or class, or the work might be similar, depending on the management of the school. If you are working as a nursery nurse in a nursery class where you carry out much the same role as a teacher, these are the main differences:

■ Responsibility: teachers have responsibility for the curriculum and for reporting, planning and so on, even if these activities are shared by all the staff.
■ Hours: teachers will work longer hours at peak times of the year, such as the report writing season, parent consultation evenings and so on.
■ Career: if you are ambitious and looking for promotion, perhaps to head teacher, you need to be a qualified teacher.
■ Pay: you will earn more as a teacher than as a nursery nurse or assistant. See the section on pay, on page 59, for details.

WHAT QUALITIES AND SKILLS WILL YOU NEED?

Liz explains what qualities she feels people need in order to do this work:

■ 'You need to be a creative person, not just artistically - creativity comes into all aspects of the curriculum. You need to like a challenge, to be adaptable, and to take a part in the creative life of the school.'
■ 'You need a sense of humour.'
■ 'You must be able to get on well with adults as well as children. You need to get on with the team and parents and other agencies, such as speech therapists and psychologists and people from the medical professions; also with volunteers in the school and other staff.'
■ 'You need to have good organisational skills: with this age group, if you're not totally organised in advance, the children won't have a good learning experience. For instance, you can't ask them to sharpen their own pencils, as you can with older children. Everything has to be done in the teacher's brain first. You learn how to do the

organisation, but to be an organised person might be something you're born with.'

■ 'You must be a flexible person who's prepared to change and adapt as you go along. There's a lot of change in early years now – the government is putting a lot of money into early years in the hope of more wraparound care, so there are a lot more initiatives. You need to be flexible with external ideas, as well as in school, which means looking at your practice and improving and changing it.'

She adds her own personal list of the good and the bad things about the job:

■ Good bits: 'job satisfaction: seeing the children change and develop, and the enjoyment of working in a team. It's never boring. I can see it might be boring as a mother at home with children, but in a school with other people's children interacting, they're never the same day by day, they are so fascinating and have such complex minds. Everything you're teaching them is interesting, not dull. You can do all the nice things.'

■ Not-so-good bits: 'all the staff clean up sick and change bottoms; there's a lot of lifting and carrying apparatus and equipment. You can't be too fastidious. We've all got things we can't handle: bottoms, sick, noses – there's a strong physical care element to it. (This is at about the same level as in a reception class – it's very physical there as well – and with less help.) You need to be quite fit physically. The amount of paperwork and administration involved is increasing year by year, but from my point of view, to teach young children is the happiest situation.'

GETTING IN

Before you can teach in a state school you need to have Qualified Teacher Status (QTS). You can get this via two main routes, outlined below. Both involve university-level study and blocks of experience in schools:

■ You can do a four-year teaching degree. This gives you a BEd (Bachelor of Education) and is taught full-time within a university.

You'll need A-levels or equivalent qualifications to get a place. QTS allows you to teach children of any age, but you will specialise in early years or primary when you apply for your course. If you are already trained in secondary school teaching you will probably have to take a conversion course to primary/early years.

■ You can gain a degree in any subject and then take an additional year learning to become a teacher, gaining a Postgraduate Certificate of Education (PGCE). This is the equivalent to the BEd in terms of educational level, but there is some feeling that doing the PGCE after a degree doesn't give enough hands-on experience. As one senior teacher says: 'I wouldn't recommend PGCE for working with young children, because I don't think that one year is a long enough training to work with this age group.' This is because, if you do the four-year BEd course, you spend time in schools throughout the four years and gradually acquire skills and experience. If you opt for the PGCE, you only have one student-year's experience of teaching. You might, though, already have enough experience. Some nursery nurses go on to train as teachers and clearly have plenty of experience with early years. You might have other, relevant, experience. When you go for jobs you might be asked why, if you want to teach nursery age, you didn't opt for the BEd route. It's worth thinking about how you might answer that before you choose your training route.

Your first year of teaching is known as your probationary year, when you are supervised by a mentor who will both help you and assess your progress.

In addition to these two main training options there are various other courses allowing you to gain QTS, such as shortened, part-time and subject conversion courses. There are also schemes such as the graduate teacher programme and the registered teacher programme, which are employment-based routes aimed at attracting mature teachers into secondary teaching and provide a teaching salary during training. These mostly apply to teaching older children.

Because of the government's emphasis on providing more early years education and care, there are new courses opening up that specialise in training early years teachers. Those that are aimed at primary level may allow you to specialise by dropping one of your subject specialisms. At the time of writing, teacher training institutions are seeing a large increase in application numbers for courses in both primary and secondary teaching.

Before applying you'll need to do your own research. A useful starting point is a book such as *Getting into Teaching* by Jeff Riley (published by Trotman). Others will also be available in your careers library or bookshop.

A NOTE ON THE NATIONAL CURRICULUM AT THE EARLY YEARS STAGE

The early years section of education is now known as the early years/foundation stage. This runs from the age of 3 until the end of the school reception year (age 5 or 6 depending on birthday). Early learning goals set out the learning and development skills most children should have achieved by the end of the school reception year. After the foundation stage, children enter the 'key stages.' These are Key Stage 1 for ages 5–7, Key Stage 2 for ages 7–11, and so on.

PAY

If you are employed by the local authority in a state school your pay is set by agreed pay scales, and even though you won't get rich teaching, it is a liveable salary for most people. Teachers start on at least £15,000 per annum, which is point 1 of the pay scale. You'll get more if you have a good degree: if you have a 2:2 degree or better you'll start on point 2, which is around £16,000. Every year you gain an additional point, up to point 9 when you'll earn £24,000. From there, pay scales get more complicated and take performance and other issues into account. Head teachers can earn up to about £75,000, but this depends on the size of the school and no nursery school head teacher would reach that level because of that size constraint.

Scottish teachers are currently celebrating, having been awarded a huge pay rise by the Scottish Assembly. Whether this will filter south is a question other teachers are eagerly asking. There are also financial incentives across the country to get people into teacher training and back into teaching after a break. These involve schemes such as waived course fees, plus training salaries of £6000 for the PGCE year. Some secondary subject teachers also receive bonuses at the start of their second year of teaching. However, these schemes don't currently apply to BEd students; they apply only to PCGE students. You need to find out about the current position by talking to your local teaching department, your careers teacher or adviser, or going onto the DfEE website.

Chapter 10
YOUTH WORKER

Once young people stop needing continual supervision and direction from adults, they need more time with their peers, developing at their own pace away from overly structured activities and organisations. The Youth Service aims to allow young people to do that by providing a range of places where they can go, activities that they may want to get involved in, and back-up services for times that get too difficult.

The Youth Service is made up of many organisations, often set up and run by volunteers, and including well-known groups such as Scouts and Guides through to small local organisations with specialist aims. There is funding available to allow these organisations to do their work, but they are generally short of cash, so many youth workers start their careers working for free and pick up experience that way. Other organisations are run by local authorities or other agencies.

Many projects are designed to stop young people from getting into trouble with the police. Some 'outreach' youth workers look for homeless or at-risk young people and help them return to their families or find a safe environment for them.

THE WORK

There is no one 'youth career' – the range is enormous. You might become employed through the local authority's youth provision, but it's more likely that you'll become a part-time and then hopefully a full-time paid officer of a voluntary-sector organisation. Your work could be anything from putting together a new football team during evenings and weekends, or doing the administration or caretaking of a youth club. It's something you need to get experience of, and often something you'd only think of doing if you already had experience of receiving these services as a youngster, or of helping to run them voluntarily. There's a lot of information on the Internet about various strands of work – see the Further Information section for starting points for research.

CASE STUDY

Oscar is 22 and works as an outreach worker with a project aimed at getting in touch with young people who are, or may become, disaffected: 'I work antisocial hours – the hours the kids are on the streets, so that's evenings and nights, Fridays and Saturdays, also some days at the youth club, after-school activities and sports.' His role is to talk to any young people who want to. 'I just hang around. People are interested, because they want to know who you are and what you're doing. At first they were wary but I just sat around and watched and talked to anyone who came near me and now I'm part of the furniture.'

He has plenty of experience through his own local youth club when he was a teenager, and helping later on. 'I know what it's like,' he says. 'I know what they're thinking, what they're gong to say half the time. There are surprises too. But they know I'm one of them, just a bit older. This would be harder if I hadn't been through it all myself.' Oscar had a difficult time in his teens, and wants to help others who are going through the same sorts of problems: 'I don't think I'll ever be totally accepted, but that's all right. They ask me stuff they can't ask at school or home. They trust me enough to ask me, but maybe not enough to tell me everything.'

He feels his role is to be there if he's needed. He's helped several young people sort out problems with their families, and talked a lot about drugs and crime, too. He hopes to do more work with the youth service, hopefully in a full-time post soon.

TRAINING

Most full-time youth workers have a certificate or diploma in youth and community work, gained through a two-year higher education course. To attract people into the work who don't want to spend two or more years in full-time education, some employers run work-based training schemes.

Part-time workers and volunteers should also be trained – at entry level, this training will probably be compulsory.

CHANGES IN YOUTH WORK

There's a new government service called Connexions that aims to pull together all the services for young people, such as the youth service and the careers service. See the website for information on how this is developing and opportunities arising from the new structure (look in Further Information, page 70). Connexions brings a new professional role, that of a personal adviser, to make it simpler for young people to access the help and opportunities that are available but, because of the fragmented structure of the youth service and other providers, are sometimes hard to find. Personal advisers will all be experienced, but will come from a wide range of backgrounds. See Chapter 11, page 66, for more on personal advisers.

PAY

You might be paid £13,000–£20,000, with more for management roles. Before you get near paid work, though, you will already have done plenty of voluntary work, probably within one or more non-profit organisations.

Chapter 11
OTHER WORK WITH CHILDREN

There are many different jobs that involve working with children. Some are listed here, with brief descriptions and information on where to go for more details.

AU PAIR

Au pairs are usually untrained, single young people who travel to another country to work part-time as childcarers and domestic helpers. You can go to any country in the European Community or another country that has an agreement to allow people to work with an au pair visa – this is different from a standard work permit: it allows only those limited hours and also a limited period of work, usually a maximum of two years.

You should have at least two full days off each week, and be provided with meals, an allowance and your own room. You will spend some of your spare time studying the language of the country you are visiting. Although this is a good way to gain experience of working with children and also to see another culture, you need to ensure that you won't be exploited; you should not be asked to work too many hours or in poor conditions, or look after babies and small children when you are not qualified or experienced to do this. Go through an established au pair agency and ensure that they find you a good family that they have used before. It's important to use a good agency to minimise any danger to you as a young person abroad on your own. You'll be paid a small allowance and your board. It can be fun and a great way to meet people if it all works out well. Contact the same agencies that place nannies – see Further Information under the nanny chapter.

EDUCATION WELFARE OFFICER

These are qualified social workers who deal with problems that prevent school children from getting the most from their education. They often work with the whole family providing a supportive role between the child's home and school. Research this role through the social work chapter contacts in Further Information.

MATERNITY NURSE

These are usually experienced nannies, though are sometimes qualified nurses, midwives or health visitors. They live with a family for a few weeks to a few months after a new baby is born, usually sleeping with the baby at night to allow the parents to sleep. Some maternity nurses come into the family home during the daytime or night-time only. You must be very experienced with babies, responsible, and good with all ages as the role involves integrating into a family at a stressful time, and may include helping teach the parents to care for the baby. Talk to nanny agencies about this work.

MOTHER'S HELP

Mother's helps are similar to au pairs in that they are not usually qualified or expected to look after small children. They go into a home and help with the chores or entertaining the children while the parent is there, or might babysit while the parent goes out for a short while. It's a good way to prepare for nursery nurse training or becoming a nanny, as you can work part-time and use the rest of your time to study, gaining relevant experience at the same time. Look for advertisements in the local paper or contact an agency or your local EYDCP.

OUT-OF-SCHOOL CLUB WORKER

Out-of-school clubs provide care before and after school. You can work here part-time while you study, and gain useful childcare experience. You may also get work in the school holidays in the same out-of-school club, or in the holidays these might transform into playschemes – see Chapter 6 on playwork. You might do both, and take the children from the out-of-school club to the playscheme in much the same way as you would to school during term time. Contact your local EYDCP for details of local clubs or the play unit at your local authority.

PERSONAL ADVISER

This is a new role under the government's Connexions service, which pulls together all youth facilities such as the youth service and the careers service to ensure that young people will have access to the help they are entitled to. Personal advisers will work in schools, colleges and the community giving advice and support, monitoring, and working with others, such as teachers and parents. The new role will develop from April 2001 and will attract people such as teachers, social workers and careers advisers, but will also train unqualified, though experienced, people into the role. See the Connexions website, listed under Further Information (page 79).

PLAYGROUP ASSISTANT

Playgroups provide childcare in short sessions for ages 3 to 5, though some take children from the age of $2\frac{1}{2}$. They provide structured play in groups, and encourage parents to be involved as volunteer workers. Most playgroups are run on a self-help basis by groups of parents with one or two paid staff. A few are run by local authorities. Playgroups are decreasing in number as more parents require wraparound care; they are still employers of a small numbers of child carers, though. You might get into this work by starting as a parent volunteer and then become part-time and study for a qualification before becoming a supervisor. They also provide good opportunities to gain initial voluntary experience with children, for young people who are thinking of working with children, but note that most playgroups only operate in school term times.

SPORTS DEVELOPMENT WORKER

You'll work with people of every age, promoting sports to the local community. Although this work does involve contact with children, if you want to work wholly with children you should consider playwork, which involves sports. Contact SPRITO for more details – see Further Information (pages 75–76).

TEACHING ASSISTANT

All schools and nursery schools employ assistants to support teachers with the learning of basic skills, especially reading, writing and maths. You'll assist in many ways, helping prepare activities, working with individuals and small groups, clearing away, and so on. You may be assigned to one class of young children; classes for older children often share assistants. There may also be work with one child who has special needs and who you help either full or part time within school. You don't usually need qualifications for this work. See the local press, or contact your local schools or your local authority.

GLOSSARY

Baseline assessment teachers assess each child starting school to see what skills and abilities are already in place, which helps them plan and measure progress. It includes assessment of language, reading, maths and social skills.

Children Act 1989 an Act to reform the law relating to children; to provide for local authority services for children in need and others; to amend the law with respect to children's homes, community homes, voluntary homes and voluntary organisations; to make provision with respect to fostering, child minding and day care for young children and adoption; and for connected purposes.

Curriculum a set programme of activities for learning.

DfEE – Department for Education and Employment the government department that looks after these areas. If you want information on any education topic, you'll find it through the DfEE website (www.dfee.gov.uk) though it might be in formal language. There are links to other websites.

Early learning goals these set out the learning and development skills most children should have achieved by the end of the school reception year.

Early Years Development and Childcare Partnerships (EYDCPs) these are locally run and act as a link between all the early years providers and users in the area, in all sectors (voluntary, private and statutory). Other aims include developing training for people working with the early years, so they're a good point of contact to find out what's happening. They are listed in the phonebook under the name of your local authority.

Education Action Zones areas or groups of schools that receive additional funding to raise standards.

Local Education Authority looks after the education for children of school age, early years, the youth service and adult education in your area.

National Curriculum sets out what children aged up to 16 in state schools should learn. See also: curriculum

OFSTED – Office for Standards in Education inspects state-funded schools and also now inspects some early years care facilities such as childminders.

SEN - Special Educational Needs learning difficulties for which a child needs additional help.

Workplace this means where you work, but not necessarily literally: it can mean the whole world of work, in phrases such as 'the modern workplace'.

Wraparound care morning to evening childcare and education allowing parents to go to work full-time.

FURTHER INFORMATION

For more information on careers in childcare generally, contact:

- Your school careers teacher and library – ask your form teacher if you don't know who this is/where to go.
- Your local careers office, adviser and library – ask your careers teacher, or look under 'careers' in the phone book; see the student's union board/officer.
- Your JobCentre (if over 18 and going into work not education) – look under 'employment services' in the phone book.
- Your local TEC/LEC – ask your careers adviser if the TEC/LEC can help you, and how to get in touch. (NB: as from 2001, in Wales contact your local Council for Education and Training – CETW).
- Your Early Years Development and Childcare Partnership (EYDCP). They are listed in the phonebook under the name of your local authority.

There may be a course available to you, free of charge, that looks at choices in working with children. This wouldn't give you a qualification but would introduce you to the various types of work available and tell you about the education you need, the training and so on. It will also inform you about health requirements, police checks for previous convictions, etc. Ask your careers adviser or contact your local Partnership (EYDCP – see above).

Some websites as starting points for research about childcare careers

Department for Education and Employment: www.dfee.gov.uk. (Try specifically: www.dfee.gov.uk/childcarejobs/what/content.html)

For careers and qualifications in Scotland: http://www.scotland.gov.uk

General careers website with lots of links: www.careers-portal.co.uk

For specific information about training and qualifications in childcare

Early Years National Training Organisation
Pilgrim's Lodge
Holywell Hill
St Albans
Herts AL1 1ER
Tel: 01727 738300
www.early-years-nto.org.uk

The Qualifications and Curriculum Authority (QCA)
29 Bolton Street
London W1Y 7PD
Tel: 020 7509 5555
www.qca.org.uk
www.accac.org.uk for Wales
www.ccea.org.uk for Northern Ireland

Scottish Childcare and Education Board
6 Kilford Crescent
Dundonald
Kilmarnock KA2 9DW
Tel: 01563 850440

The Scottish Qualifications Authority (SQA)
Epic House
28–32 Cadogan Street
Glasgow G2 7LP
Tel: 0141 226 4355
www.sqa.org.uk

The awarding bodies for childcare qualifications

You probably don't need the detailed information these awarding bodies provide when you are first researching careers – the organisations above will give you a good overview.

City & Guilds of London Institute [awards qualifications at levels 2, 3, 4]
1 Giltspur Street
London EC1A 9DD
Tel: 020 7294 2468
www.city-and-guilds.co.uk

The Council for Awards in Children's Care and Education (CACHE)
[awards qualifications at levels 2, 3, 4]
8 Chequer Street
St Albans
Herts AL1 3XZ
Tel: 01727 847636
www.cache.org.uk

Edexcel (formerly BTEC) [awards qualifications at levels 2, 3]
Stewart House
32 Russell Street
London WC1B 5DN
Tel: 0870 240 9800
www.edexcel.org.uk

Montessori Centre International [does not use the NVQ system]
18 Balderton Street
London W1Y 1TG
Tel: 020 7493 0165
www.montessori.ac.uk

Open University [awards qualifications at levels 2,3]
Walton Hall
Milton Keynes
Bucks MK7 6AA
Tel: 01908 659314
www.open.ac.uk

Oxford, Cambridge and RSA [awards qualifications at levels 2, 3]
Westwood Way
Coventry CV4 8JQ
Tel: 02476 470033
www.ocr.org.uk

Government training schemes

Modern Apprenticeships: freephone learndirect on 0800 100 900 who
will put you in touch with your local Careers Service.
www.dfee.gov.uk/mapintro.htm

New Deal Information Line, Tel: 0845 606 2626
www.newdeal.gov.uk

CHAPTER BY CHAPTER

Childminder

National Child Minding Association (NCMA)
8 Masons Hill
Bromley
Kent BR2 9EY
Tel: 020 8464 6164

Freephone information line (for parents, registered childminders and
local authority workers) 0800 169 4486 Monday and Friday 2pm – 4pm;
Tuesday and Thursday 10am – noon, 2pm – 4pm
www.ncma.org.uk

Scottish Childminding Association
Stirling Business Centre
Wellgreen
Stirling FK8 2DZ
Tel: 01786 445377

Contact your Local Authority Social Services Department on local
information about registering to become a childminder.

Hospital play specialist

Contact the National Association of Hospital Play Specialists. For general information and advice send SAE to:

Jackie Ellis
Fladgate, Forty Green
Beaconsfield
Bucks HP9 1XS
www.nahps.org.uk

Nanny

Professional Association of Nursery Nurses (PANN)
2 St James' Court
Friar Gate
Derby DE1 9BR
Tel: 01332 343029
www.pat.org.uk

For a copy of the pack 'All you need to know about working as a nanny' send a cheque or postal order for £5 made payable to PAT (PANN is part of the Professional Association of Teachers), or order by phone with a credit card.

Private residential fee-paying colleges for nannies:

Chiltern Nursery Training College
16 Peppard Road
Caversham
Reading
Berks RG4 8LA
Tel: 0118 947 1847
www.chilterncollege.com

Norland College
Denford Park
Hungerford
Berks RG17 OPQ
Tel: 01488 682252
www.norland.co.uk

Princess Christian Nursery Training College
26 Wilbraham Road
Fallowfield
Manchester M14 6JX
Tel: 0161 224 4560
www.pcnanny.com

A guide for parents thinking of employing a nanny can be obtained from:

DfEE Publications
PO Box 5050
Annesley
Nottingham
NG15 0DL
Tel: 0845 602 2260
email: dfee@prologistics.co.uk

ABTA, the Association of British Travel Agents, for finding addresses of
tour companies: www.abtanet.com

Nursery nurse

National Day Nurseries Association
Tel: 01484 541641
www.ndna.org.uk

PANN – as above in nanny chapter.

Pre-school Learning Alliance: links 17,000 community-based pre-schools
Tel: 020 7833 0991
www.pre-school.org.uk

Playworker

National Training Organisation for Sport, Recreation and Allied
Occupations (SPRITO) – has a specialist playwork unit to develop
education training and qualifications for playworkers, for children aged
5–15.

SPRITO Playwork Unit
24 Stevenson Way

London NW1 2HD
Tel: 020 7388 7755
www.playwork.org.uk

Pre-school visitor

www.surestart.gov.uk – to improve services for children under 4 and
their families in disadvantaged areas. See your phone book or call your
local EYDCP for local contacts.

Social work

The Central Council for Education and Training in Social Work
(CCETSW):

England: CCETSW Information Service
Derbyshire House
St Chad's Street
London WC1H 8AD
Tel: 020 7278 2455

Scotland: CCETSW Information Service
5th floor, 78/80 George Street
Edinburgh EH2 3BU
Tel: 0131 220 0093

Wales: CCETSW Information Service
2nd floor, South Gate House
Wood Street
Cardiff CF1 1EW
Tel: 01222 226 257

Northern Ireland: CCETSW Information Service
6 Malone Road
Belfast BT9 5BN
Tel: 01232 665 390

Community Service Volunteers (CSV):
CSV Head Office
237 Pentonville Road

London N1 9NJ
Tel: 020 7278 6601
email: information@csv.org.uk

CSV Scotland
Wellgate House
200 Cowgate
Edinburgh EH1 1NQ
Tel: 0131 622 766
email: clairetevens@csvscotland.net.com

CSV Cymru Wales
4th Floor, Aribee House
Greyfriars Road
Cardiff CF1 3AE
Tel: 02920 666737
email: csvcymru@dialpipex.com

Young Help Belfast
23–31 Waring Street
Belfast BT1 2DX
Tel: 028 9056 0120
email: younghelp@dnet.co.uk

Freephone Hotline 0800 374991
www.csv.org.uk

Teacher of early years children

A recommended book is *Getting into Teaching* by Jeff Riley, published by Trotman, ISBN 085660 5360.

Teaching Information Line (run by the Teacher Training Agency), Tel: 01245 454454.

Teacher Training Agency: www.teach-tta.gov.uk/teach

Applying for places:

Graduate Teaching Training Registry – for graduate places
Rosehill
New Barn Lane

Cheltenham
Glos GL52 3LZ
Tel: 01242 544788
www.gttr.ac.uk

National Union of Teachers
Mabledon Place
London WC1H 9BD
Tel: 020 7388 6191
www.teachers.org.uk

Scotland: The Scottish Executive Education Department (SEED)
Ss13, Area 2A
Victoria Quay
Edinburgh EH6 6QC
Tel: 0131 244 7930
www.scotland.gov.uk/teaching

UCAS (Universities and Colleges Admissions Service) – for
undergraduate places
Rosehill
New Barn Lane
Cheltenham
Glos GL52 3LA
Tel: 01242 222444
www.ucas.com

Wales: The National Assembly for Wales
Cardiff Bay
Cardiff CF99 1NA
Tel: 029 20 989200
www.wales.gov.uk

Youth worker

For England: National Youth Agency
17–23 Albion Street
Leicester LE1 6GD
Tel: 0116 285 3700
www.nya.org.uk

For Northern Ireland: Youth Action Northern Ireland
Hampton
Glenmachan Park
Belfast BT4 2PJ
Tel. 01232 760067
www.youthcouncil-ni.org.uk

For Scotland: Community Learning Scotland
(formerly Scottish Community Education Council)
Rosebery House
9 Haymarket Terrace
Edinburgh EH12 5EZ
Tel: 0131 313 2488
www.communitylearning.org

For Wales: Wales Youth Agency
Leslie Court
Lon-y-Lyn,
Caerphilly CF83 1BQ
Tel: 01222 880088
http://wya.newi.ac.uk

Other work with children

Out-of-school provision:

Kids' Clubs Network
Tel: 020 7512 2112
www.kidsclubs.co.uk

Personal adviser:

This is a new role – see the Connexions website for the latest
information: www.connexions.gov.uk

Playgroups:

The Pre-school Learning Alliance links 17,000 community-based
pre-schools.

Pre-school Learning Alliance
69 Kings Cross Road

London WC1X 9LL
Tel: 020 7833 0991
email: pla@pre-school.org.uk

Scottish Pre-school Play Association
14 Elliot Place
Glasgow G3 8EP
Tel: 0141 221 4148

Sports development work:

SPRITO – see details under playwork, above.

GENERAL

Special needs

Find out more about working with children with special needs from:

NASEN (National Association for Special Educational Needs)
NASEN House
4/5 Amber Business Village
Amber Close
Amington
Tamworth
B77 4RP
Tel: 01827 311500
www.nasen.org.uk/mainpg.htm

Jobhunting

FRES (Federation of Employment and Recruitment Agencies)
36–38 Mortimer Street
London W1N 7RB
Tel: 020 7323 4300

For a small fee, will provide a list of member nanny and au pair agencies
– also available on the Internet: www.fres.co.uk

Local government jobs: www.jobsgopublic.co.uk; www.lgjobs.com

Teaching vacancies: www.aft.co.uk

Email groups

These allow you to join free and chat with people with similar interests; they also provide links to useful sites.

UKplayworkers@egroups.com
UKplayworkersVacancies@egroups.com
UKpre-schoolgroups@egroups.com
UKtoddlergroups@egroups.com

Miscellaneous websites and helplines

BBC Education Website: www.bbc.co.uk/education

CAPT (Child Accident Prevention Trust) – dedicated to preventing accidental death and injury to children:

Child Accident Prevention Trust
18–20 Faringdon Lane
London EC1R 3HA
Tel: 0117 608 3828

Childcare Link: DfEE initiative for childcare information and vacancies, Tel: 0800 960296, www.childcarelink.gov.uk

Childcare Now! Information, advice and articles on pregnancy, child development, childcare and education, www.child-care.co.uk

Childcare Partnerships Forum: for childcare organisations to be in touch with each other, www.childcare-partnerships.co.uk/

Community Service Volunteers' National Network Hotline, Tel: 0800 374991, www.csv.org.uk

Daycare Trust – charity promoting high quality affordable childcare:

Daycare Trust
Shoreditch Town Hall Annexe
380 Old Street
London EC1V 9LT
Tel: 020 7739 2866
www.charitynet.org/~DaycareTrust

DfEE (Department for Education and Employment) Early Years Childcare Line, Tel: 0800 996600

LearnDirect – free impartial training advice and information, Tel: 0800 100900

National Early Years Network – provides practical support to childcare and early years workers:

77 Holloway Road
London N7 8JZ
Tel: 020 7607 9573
email: NationalEarlyYearsNetwork@compuserve.com

National Grid for Learning: learning on the Internet www.ngfl.gov.uk.

www.ukparents.co.uk advice on a range of child care issues.

INDEX OF OCCUPATIONS

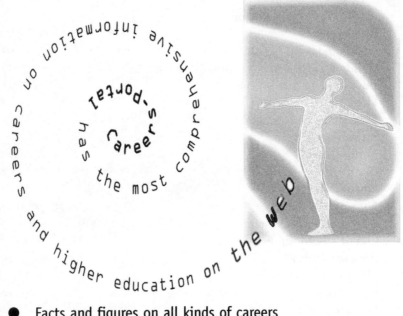

André Gide and Curiosity

Victoria Reid

Rodopi

AMSTERDAM - NEW YORK, NY 2009

Cover illustrations and design: Hugues Blondet & Victoria Reid.

The paper on which this book is printed meets the requirements of
'ISO 9706: 1994, Information and documentation - Paper for documents -
Requirements for permanence'.

Le papier sur lequel le présent ouvrage est imprimé remplit les prescriptions
de 'ISO 9706: 1994, Information et documentation - Papier pour documents -
Prescriptions pour la permanence'.

ISBN: 978-90-420-2726-8
E-Book ISBN: 978-90-420-2727-5
© Editions Rodopi B.V., Amsterdam - New York, NY 2009
Printed in The Netherlands

Acknowledgements

For financially supporting this research, I am grateful to grants from the University of Reading Research Endowment Trust Fund, the Arts and Humanities Research Council (then Board) and the University of Glasgow Faculty of Arts Strategic Research Fund.

Thank you to The Henry Moore Foundation for permission to reproduce the images at the opening and close of the text.

The book is indebted to the following people, who, in various combinations and measure, provided me with good teaching, access to sources, references, proof-reading and rich moral support: Elizabeth Boa, Caroline Cathcart, Peter Fisher, Emma Forbes, Catherine Gide, Elizabeth Gilchrist, Angelica Goodden, Alain Goulet, Danny Haikin, Joanne Lee, Magali Le Mens, Diane Lüscher-Morata, Kate Marsh, Pierre Masson, Brigid McLaughlin-Russo, Morag Moffat, Laura Mulvey, Nigel Murphy, Peter Noble, Jonny Patrick, Gregory Platten, Noël Peacock, Emily Read, Keith Reader, Walter Redfern, Innes Reid, John Reid, Jim Simpson, Pascale Stacey, David Steel, David Walker, Jo Yates, Eral Yilmaz and Paul Ziolo. Thank you, all. Last and most, my thanks go to Naomi Segal for her stimulating, rigorous and intensely generous doctoral supervision.

This book is for Hugues Blondet, *curieux de métier*.

Contents

Abbreviations

BAAG	*Bulletin des amis d'André Gide*
Corr Gide–MA	*Correspondance André Gide–Marc Allégret, 1917–1949*, ed. by Jean Claude and Pierre Masson (Paris: Gallimard, 2005)
Corr Gide–mère	*Correspondance avec sa mère 1880–1895*, ed. by Claude Martin and Henri Thomas (Paris: Gallimard, 1988)
Corr Gide–Valéry	*Cahiers André Gide: Correspondance avec Paul Valéry, 1890–1942*, ed. by Peter Fawcett (Paris: Gallimard 2009)
CPD I–IV	Maria Van Rysselberghe, *Les Cahiers de la petite dame*, 4 vols (Paris: Gallimard, 1973–77)
Désir	*Le Désir à l'œuvre, André Gide à Cambridge 1918, 1998*, ed. by Naomi Segal (Amsterdam: Rodopi, 2000)
DI–II	Jean Delay, *La Jeunesse d'André Gide*, 2 vols (Paris: Gallimard, 1956–57)
EGCaves	'Edition génétique des *Caves du Vatican* d'André Gide', CD-Rom, ed. by Alain Goulet and Pascal Mercier (Paris: Gallimard, 2001)
EC	André Gide, *Essais critiques*, ed. by Pierre Masson (Paris: Gallimard, 1999)
EPV	Alain Goulet, *André Gide: écrire pour vivre* (Paris: José Corti, 2002)
FVS	Alain Goulet, *Fiction et vie sociale dans l'œuvre d'André Gide* (Paris: Minard, 1985)
JI	André Gide, *Journal 1887–1925*, ed. by Eric Marty (Paris: Gallimard, 1996)
JII	André Gide, *Journal 1926–1950*, ed. by Martine Sagaert (Paris, Gallimard, 1997)

Klein, *Writings I–IV*	Melanie Klein, *The Writings of Melanie Klein*, 1975, 1984, 4 vols: I, *Love, Guilt and Reparation and Other Works, 1921–1945*, 1975 (London: Karnac Books and the Institute of Psychoanalysis, 1992); II, *The Psycho-Analysis of Children*, 1932 (London: Karnac Books and the Institute of Psychoanalysis, 1992); III, *Envy and Gratitude and Other Works, 1946–1963*, 1975 (London: Karnac Books and the Institute of Psychoanalysis, 1993), IV, *Narrative of a Child Analysis*, 1961 (New York: Free Press, 1984)
MAG	Jean Schlumberger, *Madeleine et André Gide* (Paris: Gallimard, 1956)
NJP	André Gide, *Ne jugez pas*, 1930 (Paris: Gallimard, 1957)
NRFH	*La Nouvelle Revue Française: hommage à André Gide, 1869–1951* (Paris: Gallimard, 1951)
OC I–XV	André Gide, *Œuvres complètes*, ed. by Louis Martin-Chauffier, 15 vols (Paris: Gallimard, 1932–39)
PFL I–XV	*The Penguin Freud Library*, trans. by Alix and James Strachey, ed. by Angela Richards (1973–82) and Albert Dickson (1982–86), 15 vols (London: Penguin, 1990–91)
Pierre-Quint	Léon Pierre-Quint, *André Gide: l'homme, sa vie, son œuvre* (Paris: Stock, 1952)
P&P	Naomi Segal, *André Gide: Pederasty and Pedagogy* (Oxford: Oxford University Press, 1998)
Rivière I–II	Jacques Rivière, 'Le Roman d'aventure', *La Nouvelle Revue française*, 54 (1 June 1913), 914–932; 55 (1 July 1913), 56–77
RMG Corr I–II	*André Gide–Roger Martin du Gard Correspondance*, ed. by Jean Delay, 2 vols (Paris: Gallimard, 1968)

RMG JI–III	Roger Martin du Gard, *Journal*, ed. by Claude Sicard, 3 vols (Paris: Gallimard, 1993)
RMG Notes	Roger Martin du Gard, *Notes sur André Gide* (Paris: Gallimard, 1951)
R	André Gide, *Romans. Récits et Soties. Œuvres lyriques*, ed. by Yvonne Davet and Jean-Jacques Thierry (Paris: Gallimard, 1958)
RI–II	André Gide, *Romans et récits. Œuvres lyriques et dramatiques*, ed. by Pierre Masson, 2 vols (Paris: Gallimard, 2009)
S	André Gide, *Souvenirs et voyages*, ed. by Pierre Masson with contributions from Daniel Durosay and Martine Sagaert (Paris: Gallimard, 2001)
VC Introduction	André Gide, '*Voyage au Congo*, Introduction to the film', *BAAG*, 30, no. 133 (January 2002), 25–30

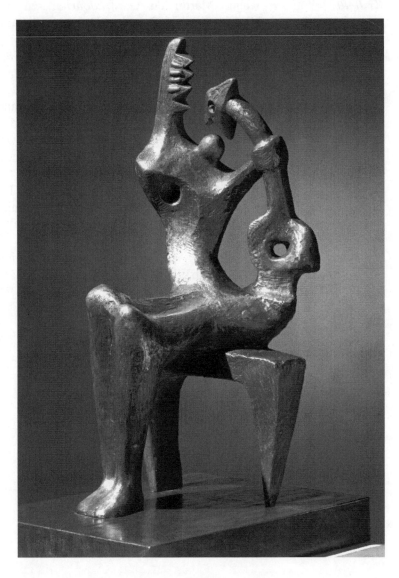

Henry Moore, *Mother and Child* (1953)
Bronze
Photo: The Henry Moore Foundation Archive
Reproduced by permission of the Henry Moore Foundation

Jules: J'envie l'ouverture de votre éventail, Jim.
Jim: O, moi je suis un raté. Le tout ce que je sais, je le tiens de mon professeur Albert Sorel. 'Que voulez-vous devenir' me demanda-t-il. 'Diplomate.' 'Avez-vous une fortune?' 'Non.' 'Pouvez vous avec quelque apparence de légitimité ajouter à votre patronyme un nom célèbre ou illustre?' 'Non.' 'Eh bien, renoncez à la diplomatie...' 'Mais alors, que dois-je devenir?' 'Un curieux.' 'Ce n'est pas un métier. Ce n'est pas *encore* un métier. Voyagez, écrivez, traduisez..., apprenez à vivre partout. Commencez tout de suite. L'avenir est aux curieux de profession. Les Français sont restés trop longtemps enfermés derrière leurs frontières. Vous trouverez toujours quelques journaux pour payer vos escapades.'

(François Truffaut, *Jules et Jim*, Screenplay, 1962)

Gide est resté fidèle à une conception que je ne saurais mieux définir qu'en disant qu'elle a constitué la pointe extrême de la curiosité de l'esprit. A une telle attitude, la curiosité devient un scepticisme qui se transforme en force créatrice.

(Klaus Mann, *Nouvelle Revue française: hommage à André Gide*,
1951)

Le voyage me lasse et je ne suis plus curieux. Las de voir, je veux faire voir aux autres, et toute ma passion se réveillera auprès d'une curiosité novice.

(André Gide, *Correspondance avec sa mère*, February 1895)

Je m'intéresse plus naturellement au développement de Michel qu'à celui de Catherine. J'ai pris ce pli, depuis ma propre enfance entourée d'admirables et vénérables figures de femmes, de considérer que la femme ne peut, sans déroger, devenir "intéressante". (Je force évidemment ma pensée, mais à peine.) Pas le temps de développer cela aujourd'hui [...] – mais c'est très important, à y revenir. Je puis avoir de l'admiration pour certains caractères de femmes; bien rarement, si pas jamais, de la *curiosité*.

(Gide, *Journal*, Christmas 1929)